MOTION

High Velocity Devotions

Kristie K. McCrary
Shari Askew . Sarah Billington . Amy Blevins .
Courtney Bodine . Aunie Brooks . Melisa Conner.
Julie M. Couch . Lesby Daniels . Angelica Garcia
. Melissa Lagrone . Missy Lares . Keylee Lederer .
Shelby Mace . Marla D. Monreal . Naomi Noy .
Jennifer L. Oldham . Khia Page . Suzette Perlmutter .
Heidi M. Pinon . Baileigh Robertson . Judith Sallador
. Rachel L. Sarmiento . Lindsey Shipman . Priscilla
Van Winkle . Cindy R. Wood . Kim Yarbrough .
Melissa Young

iUniverse, Inc.
New York Bloomington

MOTION
High Velocity Devotions

iUniverse books may be ordered through booksellers or by contacting:

iUniverse
1663 Liberty Drive
Bloomington, IN 47403
www.iuniverse.com
1-800-Authors (1-800-288-4677)

ISBN: 978-0-595-46698-6 (pbk)
ISBN: 978-0-595-48961-9 (cloth)
ISBN: 978-0-595-90994-0 (ebk)

Printed in the United States of America

Also by Velo

Velo52, Edition 1: –High Velocity Devotions:

ENDORSEMENTS

We are always blessed to discover an inspirational study on the disciplines of the soul, and Velo has compiled a delectable and insightful devotional that comforts us and encourages us to draw closer to God. Isn't that what it's all about?

Nothing is closer to the heart of God than discipleship. As our Lord instructed us, "Go and make disciples of all nations." (Matthew 28:19, NIV)

Dennis and Ginger Lindsay
President, Christ for the Nations
Women's Ministry Director, Christ for the Nations

As I turned the pages of *Motion: High Velocity Devotions*, I was taken deeper and deeper into the heart of God and into his love for me. Every devotional affirms his desire to walk in a close and intimate relationship with us. You will hear his voice speak to you through this book.

You will show me the path of life; In Your presence is fullness of joy; at Your right hand are pleasures forevermore. (Psalm 16:11, NKJV)

Elizabeth Robertson Robinson
Author, *Walking with God in the Garden; 40 Days of Prayer, Hearing God in the Garden, Expecting God in the Garden,* and *50 Days of Joyful Praise*

Take ten is a phrase used to take a break from a heavy production time. *Motion: High Velocity Devotions* brings a needed break into your daily life to take spiritual food and apply it to your life's situation. These devotions are written, in a way, to catch your heart with relevance to your daily living. Be blessed as you read these devotions and apply God's word to your life.

Joy Headley
Family Pastor, Gospel Lighthouse Church

CREATIVE TEAM

Kristie K. McCrary	Founder, Executive Director
Sheree McClure	Photography
Lesby Daniels	Contributing Editor
LeAnn Jones	Contributing Editor
Marla D. Monreal	Contributing Editor
Jennifer L. Oldham	Contributing Editor

CONTRIBUTORS

Shari Askew
Texas A & M University, College Station, Texas

Sarah Billington
Texas Wesleyan University, Fort Worth, Texas

Amy Blevins
University of Texas, Arlington, Texas

Courtney Bodine
Texas A & M University, College Station, Texas

Aunie Brooks
Southwestern Assemblies of God University, Waxahachie, Texas

Melisa Conner
University of North Texas, Denton, Texas

Julie M. Couch
Southwestern Assemblies of God University, Waxahachie, Texas

Lesby Daniels
Southwestern Assemblies of God University, Waxahachie, Texas

Angelica Garcia
Masters Commission of Dallas, Dallas, Texas

Melissa LaGrone
Southwestern Assemblies of God University, Waxahachie, Texas

Missy Lares
Southwestern Assemblies of God University, Waxahachie, Texas

Keylee Lederer
Lakeland Community College, Kirtland, Ohio

Shelby Mace
Master Commission of Dallas, Dallas, Texas

Kristie K. McCrary
Oral Roberts University, Tulsa, Oklahoma

Marla D. Monreal
Southwestern Assemblies of God University, Waxahachie, Texas

Naomi Noy
University of Akron, Akron, Ohio

Jennifer L. Oldham
Southwestern Assemblies of God University, Waxahachie, Texas

Khia Paige M. Ed
Southwestern Assemblies of God University, Waxahachie, Texas

Suzette Perlmutter
Southwestern Assemblies of God University, Waxahachie, Texas

Heidi M. Pinon
Southwestern Assemblies of God University, Waxahachie, Texas

Baileigh Robertson
Southwestern Assemblies of God University, Waxahachie, Texas

Judith Sallador
Southwestern Assemblies of God University, Waxahachie, Texas
Masters Commission of Dallas, Dallas, Texas

Rachel L. Sarmiento
Southwestern Assemblies of God University, Waxahachie Texas

Lindsey Shipman
Southwestern Assemblies of God University, Waxahachie, Texas

Priscilla Van Winkle
Southwestern Assemblies of God University, Waxahachie, Texas

Cindy R. Wood
Lee University, Cleveland, Tennessee

Kim Yarbrough
Texas A & M University, College Station, Texas

Melissa Young
Southwestern Assemblies of God University, Waxahachie, Texas

How beautiful on the mountains are the feet of the messenger
bringing good news,
breaking the news that all's well, proclaiming good times,
announcing salvation,
telling Zion, "Your God reigns!"
(Isaiah 52:7, MSG)

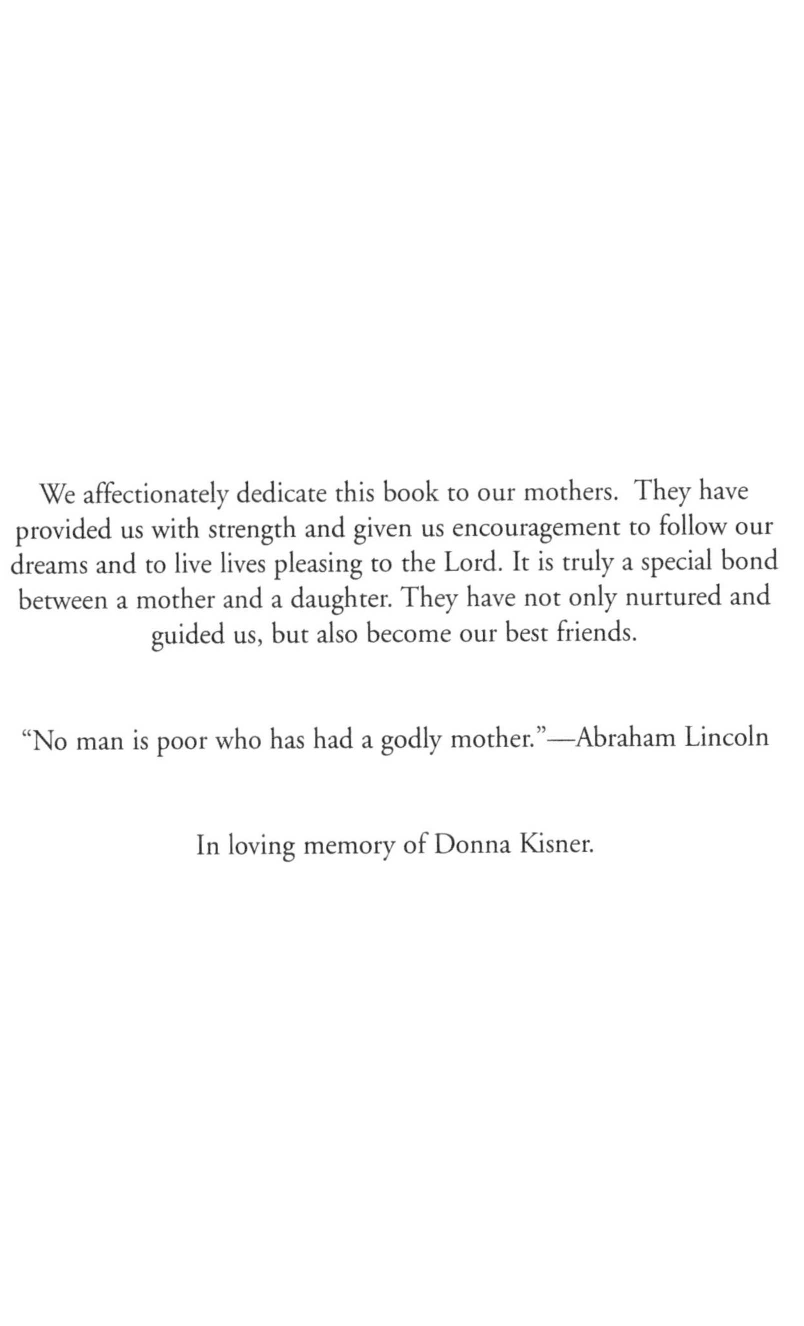

We affectionately dedicate this book to our mothers. They have provided us with strength and given us encouragement to follow our dreams and to live lives pleasing to the Lord. It is truly a special bond between a mother and a daughter. They have not only nurtured and guided us, but also become our best friends.

"No man is poor who has had a godly mother."—Abraham Lincoln

In loving memory of Donna Kisner.

Episodes

INTRODUCTION – POWERED BY VELOCITY

Our Story

Very few times in life do we plan something that actually goes better than we expect. *Velo* has been one of those life experiences for me. On August 2, 2004, I had no idea what would happen as a group of young women met in my home for the first night of our four months of Bible study. At the time it was nothing more than a short-term commitment. Nine months later, as we continued to gain velocity, I decided that if we were going to keep meeting regularly, we should have a name.

One month later, the name *Velo* was birthed as I sat on the sofa at a friend's house one Saturday afternoon. Let me take you back to my day of discovery as *Velo* received its name and it became crystal clear of our purpose and destiny as a group.

Caught in a torrential downpour, I became increasingly annoyed as I continued to search for the mystery apartment hosting the cosmetic party. Fifteen minutes late and completely drenched, I entered the front door, which lead directly into the living area. The room was filled to capacity with young ladies, making it impossible for me to avoid unwanted attention.

As I settled into the corner of the sofa, my frustration intensified as I was reminded of the thirty-minute drive back and my never ending to do list that waited patiently. Completely distracted, I was unaware that this would be the day that *Velo* would receive its name. It would also become a day that I would remember for the rest of my life.

The cosmetic consultant transitioned from the topic of make-up to fragrances. I perked up because my grandmother loved fragrances and at an early age, I caught her enthusiasm.

She began by introducing a new fragrance called *Velocity*. Immediately a light went off in my cluttered head. "*Velocity*! That word really speaks to me." I reached inside my rain soaked purse for a pen and paper and wrote down the word.

Later that evening there was a suggestion by a friend to shorten the word Velocity to *Velo*. "That's it!" I knew instantly that *Velo* was supposed to be the name of this women's organization.

Reflecting back, I see God's hand was directing me to choose the name *Velo*. It was destiny that I now more clearly understand. I had no desire to attend that cosmetic party on a rainy Saturday afternoon, yet I kept my word and went faithfully not realizing that God was going to speak to me. Velo was the perfect name for our group. When we have velocity in our lives, it changes everything. It is challenging to stay consistent in our Christian lives as young women today. We live in a world that impedes every fundamental principle of the word of God, and we need velocity in order to stay focused. When hard times come, if we have been consistent, we've gained so much velocity with God and our relationships with other Christian's that the circumstance won't shake our faith. That is what is making a difference in the lives of the members of Velo.

Around five o'clock on Monday nights, I often wonder what's going to happen, knowing that Velo will meet in two hours. Who will sit in each particular chair? Who will give her life to Christ? Who will leave with the hope and restoration that she came searching for? Regardless of my thoughts, there is one absolute: God will show up!

From a small gathering to a dynamic community of young, progressive women, Velo has experienced significant growth. We come from different cultures and creeds and share a common bond—the drive to move forward with purpose and velocity to reach and fulfill our god-given destinies.

We are members of an authentic tribe of young women who empower our generation and restore us to live lives of purpose and wellness. Our mission is simple: to provide a contemporary community that challenges today's woman to find her purpose and passion in life. By providing encouragement, direction, and relevant teaching, women's lives are enhanced and transformed.

Part of our mission is accomplished by working together to co-author inspirational books. Our first inspirational book was published in September 2006 entitled *Velo52 – High Velocity Devotions.* Now we are celebrating the publication of this book, *Motion – High Velocity Devotions.*

Whether this is the first Velo book in your collection or the second, you are going to love it because you can immediately relate and apply the life-changing principles. It is packed with real-world experiences written by ordinary people who have overcome extraordinary odds while living authentic, Christian lives.

These fifty-two timeless episodes equip you with the skills needed to balance relevance and holiness in today's world. Each episode plunges into the heart of relevant issues without hesitation and demonstrates how to navigate life, providing examples of successes and failures of others.

Motion: High Velocity Devotions is loaded with direction and hope, and you will be encouraged with every turn of the page. Inspiring, relevant, fresh—isn't that what we are all searching for?

Kristie K. McCrary
Founder, Executive Director

Please take a walk around our Web site at www.velocyte.com and learn more about Velo.

ACKNOWLEGEMENTS

Velo would like to thank some of the people who have helped to make this dream come alive, particularly Sean Wood of Slatecommunications.com and Dave Christy. We will be forever thankful to you for your belief in and support of this organization.

EPISODE 1
The Condition of Your Heart *by Kristie K. McCrary*

James and John literally left their father, Zebedee, on a boat and in the middle of the sea, kissing their joint venture business and entire family goodbye. They had probably been groomed all of their lives with the assumption that they would eventually take over. Instead, they dropped everything to follow their hearts.

Mark 4:14–20 recounts the calling of the first disciples and how the two of them actually left their father and his hired hands to follow Jesus. The Message (MSG) translation reads:

> After John was arrested, Jesus went to Galilee preaching the Message of God: "Time's up! God's kingdom is here. Change your life and believe the Message." Passing along the beach of Lake Galilee, he saw Simon and his brother Andrew net-fishing. Fishing was their regular work. Jesus said to them, "Come with me. I'll make a new kind of fisherman out of you. I'll show you how to catch men and women instead of perch and bass." They didn't ask questions. They dropped their nets and followed. A dozen yards or so down the beach, he saw the brothers James and John, Zebedee's sons. They were in the boat, mending their fishnets. Right off, he made the same offer. Immediately, they left their father Zebedee, the boat, and the hired hands, and followed.

What if James and John had stayed on their father's boat? We would never have known of them. Yet because they followed their hearts, they contributed to the most powerful and anointed book ever written: the Bible. Not to mention that they had the distinct privilege of getting to hang out with Jesus. The condition of James and John's hearts changed everything.

The condition of your heart is everything. How do you prepare your heart to seek the Lord and know his will like James and John did? Set your eyes firmly on the Lord and your purpose and destiny. When difficult decisions come or people try to confuse you and steer you the wrong direction or when you experience burnout or fear, they will not move you, because you are focused on the big picture.

What's the secret to staying focused? I believe it's momentum. When you have worked up so much momentum in your Bible reading and time with God, your circumstances will not shake you from your focus. Remember, you are the only one who can establish the condition of your heart and reach your destiny. It's completely up to you. You determine how your heart goes, and the way that your heart goes is the way that everything else will follow.

There's tremendous power behind your heart—the power of destiny and knowing that you have the maturity and ability to hear directly from God.

All twelve of the disciples were ordinary men, just like you and me. What made them different is that they chose to listen to God and follow their hearts.

> You're blessed when you get your inside world—your mind and heart—put right. Then you can see God in the outside world.
> (Matthew 5:8, MSG)

What Say You?

- Are you willing to step out of your comfort zone?
- Are you focused and listening to God's direction and destiny for your life?

EPISODE 2
Having a Mary Martha Mentality *by Cindy R. Wood*

> Now it came to pass, as they went, that he entered into a certain village: and a certain woman named Martha received him into her house.
>
> And she had a sister called Mary, which also sat at Jesus' feet, and heard his word.
>
> But Martha was cumbered about much serving, and came to him, and said, Lord, dost thou not care that my sister hath left me to serve alone? Bid her therefore that she help me.
>
> And Jesus answered and said unto her, Martha, Martha, thou art careful and troubled about many things:
>
> But one thing is needful: and Mary hath chosen that good part, which shall not be taken away from her. (Luke 10:38–42, KJV)

Y'all, as the movie says, "There's something about Mary!"

When I started learning about Jesus, all I wanted to do was sit and bask in his presence, just as she did. I spent hours on the floor, praying, worshipping, and crying my heart out to God. I wanted to be real and transparent before him. So many times I would come home from work, eat dinner, and then listen to praise and worship while talking to Jesus all night. Oh, how I loved that time! The Lord spoke to my heart, and I learned so many things by spending that time alone with him.

Wouldn't you know it? A few years later, I began to realize I was feeling spiritually empty. I would read a passage from the Bible, but I didn't study it or soak it in, because it all seemed so complicated to me. I left the explanation of scripture to the ministers on TV and to my pastor on Sunday mornings. And you know, after years of leaving it up to others, the Lord put it into my heart that it was time to get down to business. I was no longer a baby in Christ. I had grown by worshipping him, spending time in prayer, and listening to sermons, tapes, and CDs. It was time for me to step up and start seeking things out for myself.

2 Timothy 2:15 (KJV) states, "Study to show thyself approved unto God, a workman that needeth not to be ashamed, rightly dividing the word of truth." Notice the verse says, *unto God* not unto people. The Lord showed me that we don't study the Word of God just to be able to teach it to other people; we study his word so we will grow into a closer relationship with our creator. We were created to have fellowship with God and to know him and his ways. This comes by doing what Martha did: she sought his word and not just his face.

I believe now, more than ever, that we need balance in our daily lives. We need to have the spirit of Mary and Martha. Not just Mary or just Martha. We need spiritual balance. We need what I call a "Mary-Martha mentality." We need to let ourselves bask in the presence of Jesus, but also need to know his word so that when we are sitting at God's feet, we will know how to apply his word in our prayers. This mentality makes us spiritually balanced and empowers us every day of our lives.

> But those who wait on the Lord shall renew their strength; they shall mount up with wings like eagles, they shall run and not be weary, they shall walk and not faint.
> (Isaiah 40:31, NKJV)

What say you?

- Do you believe that you have reached spiritual balance in your life?
- Are your personal prayer time and Bible reading consistent?
- Would you consider yourself a Mary, a Martha, or a combination of both?

EPISODE 3
Where's the Piece I'm Looking For? *by Shelby Mace*

Wheel of Fortune was one of my favorite things to watch growing up, and it remains a favorite. Okay, call me nerdy, but I loved the challenge it presented. The whole goal of the show was to solve the puzzle as quickly as you could with as few letters as possible—and win money, of course. So basically you guessed until something fit or made sense. My sister and I competed to figure the puzzle out the quickest, and to my dismay, she always seemed to beat me at it.

One day I thought, *this is what we do with our lives.* My life could parallel the *Wheel of Fortune*. I spent so much time guessing and trying to figure out God's call and dreams for my life that I was missing the opportunity to trust God and simply relax. I tend to rationalize everything, which is not necessarily bad. When it comes to God, however, it can prevent you from getting where God wants you to go. We try to figure things out and reason with God, which only makes us frustrated. I know the end result. I know that, eventually, I will be with God. Pretty simple, huh?

I also know what God has said to me and shown me. The dilemma is the in-between, the unknown. The unknown scared me the most. I worried I might miss a step and suddenly be out of God's will or miss his best. How ridiculous is that? When I came to a critical decision in my life, my grandma used to tell me, "Shelby, go with your heart, not your head."

Oh, sure, that sounds easy. What great words of wisdom. It wasn't until I got older that I realized how much truth was in my grandma's statement and how it carried over to my walk with God.

One of my spiritual leaders, once said, "The price tag for greatness is trust." We have no choice but to trust God.

The bottom line is that you are never going to figure your life out completely. You are not the creator of the puzzle. Once you grasp this concept, you will see trusting God as a joy and stop stressing about it. It's amazing.

You may feel stuck right now, thinking that you really need to hear from God. You may even find yourself frustrated because you don't know how to hear from God.

One of my favorite sayings states, "People are born originals, but most die copies." The call of God and destiny upon your life is not a copy; therefore, the puzzle of your life is going to look different from anyone else's. You can't always take the same steps someone else is taking and expect the same results. No one else can give you the answers that you are looking for. God is not going to do things the same way in your life that he did them in someone else's.

It's easy to become agitated and feel like you're not making any progress or getting anywhere. Realize that what you do creates a piece of your puzzle. The puzzle's not already created, just floating around waiting for you to find it. So be encouraged by the fact that you don't have to solve anything; you just have to trust and rest in the one who knows every detail about your life.

> Trust in the Lord with all your heart and lean not on your own understanding; in all your ways acknowledge him, and he will make your paths straight.
> (Proverbs 3:5–6, NIV)

What say you?

- Do you find it easy or difficult to trust God?
- Could the fear of the unknown be keeping you from fully trusting in God?
- Are you trying to put the pieces of life's puzzle together with your own strength? Or, are you waiting for God to establish the big picture in his time?

EPISODE 4

The Contemplative Heart *by Lindsey Shipman*

"I do not understand what I do. For what I want to do I do not do, but what I hate I do (Romans 7:15, NIV)." The reality of Paul's words is the struggle that everyone seems to face on a daily basis. We all have an inner struggle against the greater good. There is no way to sugarcoat it, nor is there any way to run from it.

In James 4:1, James asks the question, "What causes fights and quarrels among you? Don't they come from your desires that battle within you" (NIV). There is a constant struggle between man and flesh. The problems we face can be overcome with the help of the Holy Spirit. When we allow our flesh to win, we find ourselves lost, bitter, and changed. Years ago, I wrote a poem that paints a picture of what happens when you take control, try to do it your way, and loose yourself in the midst of it all. Even though the meaning of true love is pure, true, and unfailing, I titled it, "Broken":

> I have deemed love to be a figment of the imagination, a mirage in the desert longed for and desired, but when approached, there is nothing more than distance with hollow words and empty thoughts.

It goes on to say,

> I have given everything I had to completely and utterly everything, but what I have does not please, what I have to give deceives only me, I have been deceived, broken, stained with a scarlet letter, only to be told I am not enough. Love is patient. Love is kind. So it is me, I am the deceived; I am the giver and the one without, longing to be fulfilled but empty with moments of lust.

I had given everything I felt I had to give, and it left me empty. I took ownership of making a person my focus and not my God. You will mold yourself around anything that you take ownership of. That time in my life brought much pain and bitterness, but it also brought much strength.

There really is nothing worse then feeling like Paul and doing what you hate to do. That feeling brings an unexplainable heaviness.

The burden of sin that you are carrying captivates your whole being. It brought me to a loss of vision, hope, and future. My world had to completely crash around me before I was able to say to God, "Ok, you're in control." What will it take for you?

"The Lord is close to the brokenhearted and saves those who are crushed in spirit" (Psalms 34:18, NIV). Through Christ there is fullness of joy and peace that cannot be replaced. You must let God mold you into what you were created to be. You have to "take the bull by its horns" and make it surrender to God, taming the inner beast that fights only to see you fail. You must realize that you are here for a purpose and follow God with all of your heart. In surrendering something you hold on to so tightly, you will gain more than you can ever imagine.

So whatever it is for you, whatever it is that is taking precedence over God, surrender it so that you may be whole and restored. Surrender your heart. It is the only way to live.

> Consider it pure joy, my brother, whenever you face trials of many kinds, because you know that the testing of your faith develops perseverance. Perseverance must finish its work so that you may be mature and complete, not lacking anything. (James 1:2–4, NIV)

What say you?

- What do you focus most of your time on?
- Who or what has ownership in your life?
- Is there anything in your life that you need to surrender to God?

EPISODE 5

Relying on Him *by Rachel L. Sarmiento*

October 2006 was one of the most draining months in my lifetime. Everyday, I felt that I was being tested and challenged spiritually, emotionally, and physically. I was in a midst of a battle. I battled physical exhaustion from being at work continuously for twelve plus hours at a time. I experienced so many emotions that I haven't faced for years, like feeling inadequate, depressed, lonely, worried, scared, and anxious. At times I felt so overwhelmed I didn't want to continue my relationship with God.

In my inner core, I knew that I wanted my relationship with God to be on a different level, so I forced myself to pray and read the word, but I was still doing it with my own strength, without relying on him. I remember crying several times, "God, where are you? I am here waiting, but I don't feel, hear, or see you."

During this time, I found Psalm 23, and I repeated that psalm when I woke up, on the way to work, before I went to bed, and at any free moment that I had. Finally, The end of the month came and I was physically exhausted from dealing with such an emotional roller coaster, in addition to my workload and ministry obligations. Without prior warning I walked up to my boss and said I need a week off from work. Needless to say, I was relieved when I was granted time off without notice. At last, I had a break from work and life. It was two weeks after my week off before the Lord revealed to me in an e-mail I wrote to my friend why he had given me Psalm 23 (NIV) to stand on during October.

> "The Lord is my shepherd, I shall not be in want."
>
> I realized that God is in control. He is always tender, good, and constant, not deficient with his promises.
>
> "He makes me lie down in green pastures, he leads me beside quiet waters,"
>
> God wanted me to have rest and peace.
>
> "He restores my soul. He guides me in the path of righteousness for his name's sake."
>
> I am complete with him.

> "Even though I walk through the valley of the shadow of death, I will fear no evil, for you are with me; your rod and your staff, they comfort me."

God spoke to me: "Rachel, even though you can't see all of your future ahead of you and it seems there are stressful times at work, do not be afraid. Just take my hand I am always with you."

"You prepare a table before me in the presence of my enemies. You anoint my head with oil; my cup overflows."

God said, "Rachel my child I will always bless you even though sometimes you don't feel you deserve it but you do and I will always give you more."

"Surely goodness and love will follow me all the days of my life, and I will dwell in the house of the Lord forever."

Reflecting back, I understand that God gave me this psalm to reassure me that, even though I had and will have valleys and challenges in my life, he is my shepherd. God guarantees that he will walk me through and comfort me. That October confirmed to me that God wanted me to get back to the basics of relying on him completely.

> You're blessed when you're at the end of your rope. With less of you there is more of God and his rule.
> (Matthew 5:3, MSG)

What say you?

- Have you ever experienced a time in your life when you could not hear, feel, or see God?
- During the valley times of your life, do you try to take care of everything with your own strength or do you relax and trust God?

EPISODE 6

Insignificant? Depends on Who You Ask *by Aunie Brooks*

There are many things in this world that appear insignificant at first glance, until someone of importance places a significant value on it. At first glance, a little Chihuahua appears scrawny and ugly, a mockery of a dog. But as soon as Paris Hilton wraps diamonds around its neck and places it in a $1400 Fendi canvas bag to sport as an accessory, the little tyke becomes a coveted treasure with a very expensive price tag.

Likewise, we often struggle with feeling insignificant. We are willing to spend thousands to make ourselves at least look important in an attempt to make us feel important, hoping that we will actually become important. But when the most important being of all time, the Creator of everything, places value on you, that's when you really become significant.

Take the boy who offered five loaves of bread and two fish to the disciples in the miracle of the feeding of the five thousand. This miracle is recorded in all four gospels, but John is the only one who mentions that the food came from a little boy. After all, where the bread came from does seem like an insignificant detail. Before the miracle, it was all insignificant—five loaves and two fish? When Christ asked the disciples to see what they could find to feed the crowd Philip responded, "Eight month's wages would not buy enough bread for each one to have a bite!" This could be paraphrased as, "Have you lost your mind? We don't have enough money to buy food for five thousand men, along with their wives and children."

But since you don't argue with Christ for long, the apostles began their search. When they returned to Christ, all they had to present was five small barley loaves and two small fish from a little boy—and yes, the scripture uses the adjective small; I didn't just throw that in there. Sound insignificant? I'm sure the disciples presented the food with the attitude of, "See? This is all we could find. We need to just send everyone home."

What's amazing about God is that you never have too little to offer him. How much you have has nothing to do with how big his return can be. I think the reason God had the food come from a little boy is because the boy, in and of himself, seems insignificant. Matthew, Mark, and Luke don't even mention him. After all, what do children have to offer the world? Adults take care of them. God shows us through this story that there's no person too small and no amount too small for God to perform one of the largest, most talked about miracles ever recorded.

> I can do everything through him who gives me strength. (Philippians 4:13, NIV)

What say you?

- Do you ever feel insignificant?
- Do you ever feel that what you have to offer God is of little value or significance compared to what so many others offer?

EPISODE 7
The Weakest Link *by Baileigh Robertson*

Do you remember the game show *The Weakest Link*? The concept goes a little something like this: nine contestants answer a chain of general knowledge questions. With every correct answer a bank of communal money grows. If increases, however, the bank is emptied, and all players lose any money they had previously earned. Talk about pressure.

So, while I understand that concept of the game, I never really enjoyed watching it. Have you ever felt like the weakest link in your own life? Have you ever felt like, no matter what you did or how hard you tried, you just couldn't bring as much to the table as everyone else? There have been times when I have felt that way. If you are reading this and can identify with that feeling, I have hope for you. Well, actually, hope that I found in God, who changed my life and loves me no matter what my weaknesses are.

Let me share with you the hope he's given me. I share a passage written by the apostle Paul in the Bible. See, Paul has this problem he calls a thorn. It could be many things, but, for Paul, it's definitely a thorn in his side. What's interesting is that even though he asks God to take it away, God, in his wisdom, chose not to. I find comfort in Paul's revelation.

> But he said to me, "My grace is sufficient for you, for my power is made perfect in weakness." Therefore I will boast all the more gladly about my weaknesses, so that Christ's power may rest on me. That is why, for Christ's sake, I delight in weaknesses, in insults, in hardships, in persecutions, in difficulties. For when I am weak, then I am strong. (2 Corinthians 12:9–10, NIV)

Paul realized that, though he was weak, God could use Paul's weakness to glorify himself. Paul shifted his thinking when he realized that his weakness had less to do with him and more to do with glorifying God through it. God doesn't ask us to hide our weakness by pretending we're perfect. He doesn't want us to compare our weaknesses against the strengths of others. He doesn't even always choose to strengthen our weaknesses right away.

Today, I urge you to accept that God created you in a unique way.

You are the apple of his eye, and he loves you. He created you with a special purpose that no one can accomplish as well as you can. When you understand this, you find that you are not comparing but rejoicing in each part that we all play as we advance toward his kingdom together.

I urge you to carry out the joy of 2 Corinthians 2:14–17.

> But thanks be to God, who always leads us in triumphal procession in Christ and through us spreads everywhere the fragrance of the knowledge of him. For we are to God the aroma of Christ among those who are being saved and those who are perishing...And who is equal to such a task? Unlike so many, we do not peddle the word of God for profit. On the contrary, in Christ we speak before God with sincerity, like men sent from God.
> (2 Corinthians 2:14–17, NIV)

What say you?

- Do you ever feel that you are the weakest link in your world?
- Do you trust God to be your strength in the weak moments of your life?

EPISODE 8

A New Name *by Lesby Daniels*

Our past experiences affect the future if we hold on to them.

Satan keeps us from making a new beginning in Christ. Satan messed things up for us in the past, and he likes to remind us of our mistakes daily. I have had many conversations with friends about their pasts and how they don't feel worthy of their callings. Holding onto the past keeps them from overcoming it.

I have been stuck in this very position. I didn't allow God to change me into the image of Christ and give me a new life worth living because of my past. Sometimes I still struggle with letting Christ into my life, and I have to remind myself to fight the lies of the devil. If I don't, he will destroy my future and all the amazing things the Lord has planned for me. Instead I ask myself, if I have messed up so badly, how could I be chosen to do the work of God?

God reminded me about Paul, who persecuted Christians. He had to let go of his past in order to receive his calling. He had to remind himself to forget and walk towards his future and destiny. When Paul wrote to the church of Philippi, he said, "Brothers; I do not consider myself yet to have taken hold of it. But one thing I do: Forgetting what is behind and straining toward what is ahead" (Philippians 3:13, NIV).

"Convert" is defined in Webster's dictionary as "to bring over from one belief, view, or party to another." In Acts, Saul was converted to Paul. Paul had received a new name in order to have a new and fresh start with God. He entered his future by letting go of the old man inside of him.

Christ changed what Paul believed about himself and the crimes he had committed. Paul changed his thinking.

Paul received a new name because he decided to move forward into the life that the Lord had planned for him. He released his past and everyone associated with it to God. Saul had been a persecutor, but Paul became a defender for the work of the Lord. He wrote epistles, transformed people to Christ, and took missionary journeys. The change in Paul's name showed that he was a changed man. He became a new creation, received new strength, and redirected his life.

Don't cherish negative memories from your previous life. Instead, let the love of God give you a new life, one worth living. Don't stay the same old you, let God give you a new name. Ask the Lord to show you what your new name is.

> Therefore, if anyone is in Christ, he is a new creation; the old has gone, the new has come!
> (2 Corinthians 5:17, NIV)

What say you?

- Paul was able to accept God's grace and forgiveness for his past and receive a new life and a new name. Have you accepted this same grace and forgiveness?
- Does the shame of your past define you and keep you from moving forward in God's plan for your life?
- What past failure or failures could you be holding on to?

EPISODE 9

The Big Mo *by Kristie K. McCrary*

What's the big deal with momentum? It's not tangible. You can't really see it. Dictionary.com defines momentum as a "force of speed of movement." It's the big comeback—the element that rallies a team from ten points down to win the game. Momentum is the force that empowers a mother to race into the middle of the street and save a child from an oncoming car. Now that's momentum.

We live in a world that impedes every fundamental principle of the word of God, and we need momentum in order to stay focused. Think of it like this: if you're traveling in a car at the speed of ten miles an hour, a U-turn is going to be a piece of cake. However, if you're in that same car traveling sixty, seventy, or maybe even eighty miles an hour there's no way that you can make a U-turn, because you have so much momentum. Momentum changes everything in life!

It's the same with our relationship with God. When hard times come, if we have been consistent, we've gained so much momentum with God that the circumstance won't shake our faith. A popular Christian song talks about how that we can't actually see the wind, yet we can see the effects of the wind. It's the same way with momentum. We can't see momentum, but we can see its effects.

In your relationship with the Lord, momentum takes you to the top and helps you to see positive effects in every area of your life. John says:

> Don't love the world's ways. Don't love the world's goods. Love of the world squeezes out love of the Father. Practically everything that goes on in the world—wanting your own way, wanting everything for yourself, wanting to appear important—has nothing to do with the Father. It just isolates you from him. The world and all its wanting, wanting, wanting is on the way out—but whoever does what God wants is set for eternity. (1 John 2:15–17, MSG)

Today, I want to challenge you to stay focused and consistent in your relationship with God. It will help you to gain continued momentum in your life. Develop a hunger for God, a passion for purity, and intolerance for the things of this world. Don't compromise your life with the affections of this world, because they're not lasting. The church, the world, and the future are in our hands. As a generation we need to commit to making a difference, and the only way we can accomplish change is to gain momentum in our relationship with God. Why? It's because momentum changes everything.

> Friends, don't get me wrong: By no means do I count myself an expert in all of this, but I've got my eye on the goal, where God is beckoning us onward—to Jesus. I'm off and running, and I'm not turning back.
> (Philippians 3:13–14, MSG)

What say you?

- Do you have a sincere passion for the things of God?
- Are you easily distracted by circumstances, people, and everyday life?
- Are you willing to spend significant time in the Word of God and in prayer in order to maintain momentum?

EPISODE 10

Celebrate *by Priscilla Van Winkle*

I can still smell the odd antique scent of my favorite tan dress from when I was a little girl. It had ruffle sleeves and a lace lining around the sheer fabric. I was so little that the material would drag underneath my feet when I twirled. When my mother wasn't looking, I would creep into her closet to find the tallest pair of high heels so I could reach the red rose lipstick that she kept on the marble sink. The lipstick sat just to the right of the porcelain jewelry box where she kept my grandmother's diamond ring. Sometimes, I would place the ring on my finger as I closed my eyes, believing that I was Cinderella dancing on clouds in my glass slippers. No, I was Belle in my golden dress humming a song and everyone circled around to watch me.

While daydreaming, I opened my eyes, I saw an audience of close to three hundred before me. I'm in a red silk dress, singing an all too familiar melody, "Barely even friends, then somebody bends unexpectedly." It was my junior voice recital, and nine years later, the little girl who wanted to be a princess at six was still singing the same tune.

I would only have to say one phrase in order to take you down memory lane: "Once upon a time." Were you Sleeping Beauty awakened by a kiss? Were you Rapunzel, throwing down your golden locks? Or were you like me—a brown-haired, babe-admiring Belle? I'm sure a few of the guys wanted to be Ken in his '69 mustang or Prince Charming riding in on his white stallion to save the day, but they'll never own up to it. Little do the guys know that the true superheroes are the ones who sweep us off our feet. I know that there are times I recall these memories and look back and laugh at when I so desperately wanted to become Belle, but how many times have I looked in the mirror anxiously wanting to be something I'm not? We try so hard to become princesses, but why does it seem like our dreams are in such a far away land?

I'm sure, if we changed up Cinderella's story, it wouldn't look too different from ours. Just add a few haircuts gone wrong and the countless hours Cinderella spent bleaching her hair blonde until it began to fall out.

She didn't always have the hourglass figure; it probably came from the latest diet trend. And what about that time Ken broke her heart when he dropped her for a blonde bimbo named Barbie? God created all of us to be unique, and we need to do our best to celebrate our uniqueness.

"For you created my inmost being; you knit me together in my mother's womb. I praise you because I am fearfully and wonderfully made; your works are wonderful, I know that full well" (Psalm 139:13–14, NIV). Dictionary.com defines fearfully as "full of awe." The Most High God was full of awe when he made you. You were created unique—no one who has ever walked this earth before you, and no one after you will ever have the same fingerprint, eye print, or footprint as you. The reason why our dreams seem so far off is because we don't celebrate the dream we are.

At the age of twenty-one, I'm not even a quarter of the way through my life, but if I want my end to be a happily-ever-after, I can't live my beginning in regret. The only way I can do that is by celebrating the uniqueness of every day. "Therefore do not worry about tomorrow, for tomorrow will worry about itself. Each day has enough trouble of its own" (Matthew 6:34, NIV). And don't try to write your name in the script of someone else's story. What if Cinderella had tried to be Sleeping Beauty? She would have slept through the royal ball, never would have lost her glass slipper, and there would have been no Prince Charming on a white stallion because she focused on someone else's story and missed hers. Today, celebrate your uniqueness!

> I'm just as happy with little as with much, with much as with little. I've found the recipe for being happy whether full or hungry, hands full or hands empty. Whatever I have, wherever I am, I can make it through anything in the One who makes me who I am.
> (Philippians 4:12–13, MSG)

What say you?

- Do you compare yourself to others?
- Do you celebrate your uniqueness?

EPISODE 11
True Identity *by Amy Blevins*

How many people reading this would say that they are in a place in their life where something needs to happen? You're in a rut—spiritually, emotionally, mentally, physically—and you're finally tired and ready to do something about it.

Velo's purpose statement says that we are an authentic tribe of young women who empower and restore our generation to live a life of purpose and wellness. Being authentic is the ability to be you without fear or shame. To be healthy is to separate the truth from the lies and live in the truth. The Bible says that Satan comes to kill, steal, and destroy. Outside of physical death, the fastest way to destroy a person is to steal her identity and to convince her she is something other than what God designed her to be. Satan's strategy starts in discreet ways, and if we accept his lies as truth, we're in danger of transforming into an isolated, unfruitful, and absolutely miserable person over time. That misery expresses itself in different ways.

It's easy to see a person's self-identity by her behavior. We wear our self-image like a cloak. Some of us wear unhealthy cloaks for so long they stink. The scent of the cloak becomes so familiar we don't notice; however, other people can't help but notice. We get signals that something's wrong because of the way people interact with us or do not interact with us at all.

Your demeanor is the effect of what you believe about yourself. So, what's the cause? What *truth* have you built your life around that says you aren't enough? What lies have become truth to you? The toll it takes on your spirit, your life, your career, and your personal relationships is unfathomable. If these behavioral patterns have become such a part of your life that you are scared of what your life would be without them, confess that to God. Allow him to bring these areas to light so your mind and spirit can be healed and restored to wholeness. After you confess what's in your heart, take the cloak off for the last time. Physically release the burden that you've been carrying. Once you're done with that, praise God for all he has done in your life and all that is to come, because his truth will replace every lie. His truth will set you free to live the dynamic, authentic life that he has always wanted you to live.

Others have healthy cloaks. They know who they are. They have made peace with their pasts, surrendered their futures, and know whom they serve. They trust God with their lives, serve other people rather than themselves, have thankful hearts, and possess the ability to actively love others. Are their lives perfect? Absolutely not. Are their lives favored? Yes, because they do not live unto themselves. Do other people respond favorably to them? Yes, because they respond to the joy of the Lord that is within them.

Once someone has a healthy self-image, she is capable of maturing in the attributes of a godly woman. I am fortunate that I can name several women who exhibit grace, warmth, thoughtfulness, and assurance, along with a wise spirit. They inspire me on a regular basis. But, until recently, it didn't occur to me that I could develop those attributes myself. I believed that I just wasn't born with certain strengths, so I should honor and respect them in others and try to focus on what I could do. What's missing in that belief? The Holy Spirit. For some reason, I didn't recognize the Holy Spirit's role in their maturity, self-respect, self-control, serving hearts, and other traits. I limited my maturation to what I could do on my own strength. Yet, from the day that I acknowledged Jesus as the Son of God, confessed my sins, and accepted him into my heart, I accepted another role.

God has several names that describe different aspects of his character, including the King of Kings and the Lord of Lords. As such is his name, by virtue of our spiritual birth, we are daughters of the king. That is the truth. That is real. No one can take that away from you. So, as the daughter of the king, what is possible for you? "All things are possible for those that believe." But how do we strengthen those attributes? We do so through the Holy Spirit and God's word. The Bible is our sword of truth, and it shows us what we are, what we can accomplish, and how we will accomplish it.

Thanks to God's faithfulness, not only can we give thanks for the ability to cast off the lies that Satan has convinced us of, we can now take on the cloak of who we really are—royalty in Christ as we assume our true identity.

> But you are the ones chosen by God, chosen for the high calling of priestly work, chosen to be a holy people, God's instruments to do his work and speak out for him, to tell others of the night-and-day difference he made for you—from nothing to something, from rejected to accepted.
> (1 Peter 2:9–10, MSG)

What say you?

- Do you have a healthy and balanced self-esteem?
- Do you feel that you have positive attributes?

EPISODE 12

Shine *by Angelica Garcia*

While praying Friday night at our Velo prayer gathering, the word shine came to my mind. I think we've all heard as kids the song that says, "This little light of mine, I'm gonna let it shine." It sounds silly, but we would yell "No, I'm gonna let it shine!" at the top of our lungs when we reached that part of the song.

As kids we had no shame to shine and stand up for what was right. As adults we tend to hide our belief or keep quiet and mind our own business.

While I prayed God revealed to me how he had created me so I could shine and not hide. He told me that I should never let anyone or anything keep me from shining. Sometimes we allow our surroundings to hide us and keep us from being seen. I felt in my heart that God was telling me, "You have relationships in your life that are not allowing you to shine. These relationships keep you hidden from the public, they don't encourage you, they don't have hope for their own futures and they are leading you astray." He also showed me the people who were there to help me shine, to encourage me, pray for me, and mentor me. He showed me the people I need to shine for. I know it sounds weird, but to shine means to give hope and be a light for those who are looking for hope in the darkness.

I knew exactly what God meant. I realized that I was holding on to relationships with people who were okay, but who kept me from being who God had called me to be. How can I even want to be part of anything that is not of God? I cried out to God and asked him to forgive me for wasting time and for not shining the way he wanted me to! I'm so glad that he revealed a simple verse in the Bible to me. God himself put me on a hilltop, on a light stand, to shine!

After the Lord revealed to me that he had created me to shine, I developed a confidence that I've never felt before. I felt important, beautiful, and like I could accomplish anything that he sent my way. I'm not going to let anyone keep me a secret anymore. I'm the daughter of a great king.

Don't let anyone—including yourself—keep you from shining where you are. Shine in the midst of sickness and believe that the

Lord is your healer. Shine in the midst of trouble and know that the Lord is your peace. Shine when you are weak and let God be your strength. Be encouraged and know that you were created to light your surroundings. I know that God has called me to shine and do nothing less.

> Here's another way to put it: You're here to be light, bringing out the God-colors in the world. God is not a secret to be kept. We're going public with this, as public as a city on a hill. If I make you light-bearers, you don't think I'm going to hide you under a bucket, do you? I'm putting you on a light stand. Now that I've put you there on a hilltop, on a light stand—shine! Keep open house; be generous with your lives. By opening up to others, you'll prompt people to open up with God, this generous Father in heaven.
> (Matthew 5:14–16, MSG)

What say you?

- What type of relationships do you have in your life? Are they healthy? Are they encouraging you to shine?
- Who are you shining for?
- Are you a dispenser of hope and a lamp-lighter?

EPISODE 13
Have You Ever? *by Keylee Lederer*

Have you ever had the desire to do something that you thought was totally out of reach? I know the feeling. Then one day I sat down and just started to write. I had no idea that I had the ability to write poems until I tried, and you know what? I'm sure glad I did.

The moment I heard him,
A frown became a smile;
A peek out the window became a stare;
A small walk led to a never-ending journey.

The moment I heard him,
I chose to listen.
I spoke to him again.
His answers make me glisten.
He guides my direction.
He never answers with a question.

The moment I heard him,
I felt him;
He touches my heart—
Yet that's only the start.

The moment I heard him,
I watched him die.
He hung there just for me, for us,
To take away my sins,
To forgive.
His arms are spread wide;
His body stands tall.
The width of his forgiveness crosses at his heart
Into the height of his Holiness,
Not for just one, but for all.

The moment I heard him,
I wanted him to see

A child of his I desired to be.

Do you hear him? He desires to forgive you too.

When the Lord inspires you to write, don't pass up the opportunity. He wants to speak to you through your creativity. He will guide the direction of the questions you've asked. Scriptures will repeat in your mind, and your thoughts will speak these scriptures. God will tell you who these scriptures are for—a message for you and someone else. The mind may think quickly, but your pen will write permanently.

The messages God sends you may be quick, but they will always be true. Write them down, you will need them soon. Your dreams and aspirations will pour out of your pen, coming straight from your heart. God will read your desires and feel your love for these dreams. Repeat these writings and build upon these dreams. Do not ever give up.

Have you ever had a dream? Be loyal to his guidance, listen to directions, and birth your dreams! "Talitha, cumi" (Mark 5:41, NKJV). Stand up, stay focused, and love miracles.

> Then he took the child by the hand, and said to her 'Talitha, cumi,' which is translated, 'Little girl, I say to you, arise.' (Mark 5:41, NKJV)

What say you?

- Is there a dream birthing in your life? Does your dream come from God?
- Are you listening for direction from the Lord concerning your dreams and aspirations?

EPISODE 14
Dream-Chaser *by Kristie K. McCrary*

He was born in Henryville, Indiana, on September 9, 1890. When he was six, his father's sudden death forced his mother into the workforce, and he assumed the task of preparing meals for the family. Shortly after his fortieth birthday, he began to prepare chicken for people who passed by his service station in Corbin, Kentucky. He didn't have a restaurant, so he served his chicken dinners in his living quarters behind the gas station.

Through relentless dedication, his local popularity grew, and he made the decision to move from the service station into a motel and restaurant that seated 142 people, where he began working as a chef. For the next nine years, he perfected his secret chicken recipe, blending eleven herbs and spices that would eventually make him and his fried chicken famous.

He was forced to sell his property in order to make way for Interstate 75 at the age of sixty, and knew that the loss of his restaurant had the potential to steal his chances for his lifelong dream. Rather than accept fate, in 1952, he took a hefty risk and devoted his time to building the chicken franchise, using money from his first Social Security check in 1955 to visit prospective franchise locations.

He developed a marketing strategy that would require hard work and dedication and began to travel across the country in his car, convincing restaurant after restaurant to allow him to cook batches of chicken for the owners and their employees. If they were pleased, he entered a business agreement with a handshake that would earn him the commission of one nickel for every chicken sold.

As a young man, he had always dreamed of building a successful chicken franchise, and although his dream didn't develop until he was sixty-two, he never gave up or entertained the thought that it was too late to live out his dream. Within a matter of years, his dedication, focus, and hard work paid off as his small business slowly turned into one of the largest fast-food chains in the world.

This amazing business personality, corporate icon, multimillionaire, founder, and developer of the world's famous Kentucky Fried Chicken was none other than Colonel Harland David Sanders. Colonel Sanders had a dream, and he did not ever give up. I believe he must have had a great understanding of how to follow your dreams and the extraordinary rewards of patience.

Dreams take time to birth. Just as a mother goes through a nine-month, natural birthing process, our dreams take time to birth and mature in order to come to fulfillment. The delays and birthing pains are natural and inevitable. They're also part of the process. However, when a dream finally comes into focus, it's often grander than our limited human imaginations can comprehend.

As extravagant a dream as Colonel Sanders had, I wonder if he realized that it would reach the far ends of the earth? If you wait patiently on the Lord to bring your dream to pass, it will be worth the risk and prove to be more than you expected. I believe that people who accomplish extraordinary things have a greater understanding of dreams and the risks involved in waiting patiently for them to birth.

I challenge you today: be a dream-chaser!

> What do you mean, "If I can?" Jesus asked. Anything is possible if a person believes.
> (Mark 9:23, NLT)

What say you?

- Do your dreams seem impossible?
- Do you ever dream of the possibilities of an extraordinary, above-average life?
- Are you willing to wait patiently for your dreams and not settle for the ordinary?

EPISODE 15
The Faith of Hope *by Suzette Perlmutter*

The motivational speaker, Ed Foreman says, "We change when the pain to change is less than the pain to remain as we are."

These words rang in my heart as I sat at the dinner table with some friends. Tears were streaming down my face during a discussion of my painful drama that was going on at the time. A moral crisis had happened, and I was hurt and crushed by all the details. But as I heard the words above spoken by a friend, it finally gave me the dose of truth that I needed to take life-changing steps to detangle myself from a toxic and abusive relationship.

My friend's words gave me hope. I wanted to change things more than anything, and more importantly, I wanted to change me. With his words, I glimpsed a hope that things could change, and I wanted it more than getting revenge or retribution for what had happened to me. I decided then that a hope of changing my sorrows into something better could give me a holy stubbornness, and I began standing with what I call a "faith of hope." A very well known scripture on faith says, "Now faith is being sure of what we hope for and certain of what we do not see" (Hebrews 11:1, NIV)

As I finally ended my six-year drama, I realized how much better I felt the further I was from the situation. I began to see how much happier I was. It wasn't easy, but deep down I knew I had this faith of hope that God was going to give me my heart's desire, not a curse, if I would seek him and serve him with all my heart. I looked to the needs of others and helped other women I saw going down the road I had traveled. If I could stop one girl out of a million from the life-altering pain and anguish I had felt, then it would have been worth it. I believe God helped me to counsel several women from going back to unhealthy relationships and let them see that God is always faithful. He sees our tears and desires to give us good things.

I got stronger each day, because I believed that God has a purpose and a plan and that the hope I carried was greater than the void and hopelessness I had once felt in an unhealthy relationship. I fought to bring holiness into my life again and into the lives of the young adults around me. I believed that God knew my morals were Bible-based, and he would give me a husband who carried the same ones I did. I was sure of what I hoped for.

I would find out in explicable proportions how faithful God is. I met my husband, Scott, and was engaged and married to him within about eight months. No, I don't believe it should be like that for everyone, but God wrote a love story greater than my human mind could have. The heavenly bliss I have found in my husband, I will pray for other girls to have. It has been every bit the life worth waiting for. We're not foolish enough to think we're perfect, but the happiness that we now feel makes me thankful to God every morning.

My faith of hope kept me from making a horrible mistake in my life and helped me counsel others. I pray other women will find their own faith, believing unwaveringly that there is hope. There is more. God does want to give you your husband. Believe me; it is worth waiting for. God's design is so much greater than ours.

> Delight yourself in the Lord and he will give you the desires of your heart.
> (Psalm 37:4, NIV)

What say you?

- Do you have the faith of hope?
- Do you believe that God has a purpose and plan for your life?

EPISODE 16

Not Pruning *by Shari Askew*

I had always thought that a plant was pruned because it didn't bear fruit. As many times as I have heard about the pruning process, I never thought that God would use my fifteen-year-old cousin, Tiesha, to prune me. Before she came to live with me, I had Velo girls praying for her, for me, for my mom, for my finances, for my patience, for my cousin's school, and for her friends. We ran the gamut of things to cover in prayer.

One Friday night at a prayer meeting we held at Sister Hall's house—Sister Hall was one of our prayer partners—everyone prayed for me. My prayer requests were for Tiesha and my current job situation. I had been a waitress for over three years. When my mom and I decided to bring my cousin to live with us, I knew this would require me to find a better paying job. So I went to a placement agency and received an assignment very quickly. The pay wasn't great, and there were no insurance benefits, but it was slightly better than what I had been doing. I still needed an upgrade.

The Lord gave one of my friends a word for me that was right on. However, my gut reaction was to think, "Not pruning! God, anything but pruning. Instruction I can handle; correction, even discipline and rebuke, just please don't prune me."

I knew this was going to hurt. In my mind, pruning was harsh and involved cutting away limbs that were dead or dying. Then I read John 15:2, "Every branch in Me that does not bear fruit He takes away; and every branch that bears fruit He prunes, that it may bear more fruit" (NKJV). The light came on when I read that. "Every branch that bears fruit he prunes," the ones that bear no fruit are taken away. Oh! So that means that he needs to prune me because I am bearing fruit. His pruning will cause me to bear more fruit, which will result in more pruning. All lights had come on, but then I started to wonder what kind of fruit could God possibly want me to grow. Galatians 5:22–23 tells me "the fruit of the Spirit is love, joy, peace, longsuffering, kindness, goodness, faithfulness, gentleness, self-control. Against such there is no law." (NKJV) I don't think I mind growing that kind of fruit.

Since my cousin has come to live with us there has never been a dull moment. Where I was selfish and self-centered, God has used Tiesha to switch my focus from myself and onto others. As a result of this experience, I truly feel that I want anything that is part of my lifestyle or personality that is not like God to be removed so that I can grow into a deeper relationship with Christ. I want to be made into something that I have never been before.

Pruning is never easy and none of us really ask for it. However, looking back, I realize that my experience with pruning became one of the greatest blessings of my life.

> I am the true vine, and My Father is the vinedresser. Every branch in me that does not bear fruit He takes away; and every branch that bears fruit He prunes, that it may bear more fruit.
> (John 1: 1–2, NKJV)

What say you?

- Have you ever been pruned? Do you look back now and see positive results from the pruning?
- Are there things in your life now that need to be pruned so that you will bear more fruit?

EPISODE 17

Rejection *by Julie Couch*

Rejection is such a negative feeling. No one enjoys experiencing it, yet not only does everyone experience it, but everyone causes others to experience it as well.

Rejection is looked upon as a bad thing. And in fact, it is bad when we face it. However, rejection has a positive side. Just like anything else you experience, rejection builds character, makes you who you are, and brings humility. When you experience rejection—as you go through it—you cannot see this positive side. But it is there. Rejection usually brings brokenness. It causes us to become brokenhearted, and yes, humble.

When we face rejection, God wants us to know that he is there to mend our broken hearts and broken spirits. He sends others, who have also faced rejection and have found the good in it, to help us. Isaiah 61:1–3 says:

> The Spirit of the Sovereign Lord is on me, because the Lord has anointed me to preach good news to the poor. He has sent me to bind up the brokenhearted, to proclaim freedom for the captives and release from darkness for the prisoners, to proclaim the year of the Lord's favor and the day of vengeance of our God, to comfort all who mourn, and provide for those who grieve in Zion—to bestow on them a crown of beauty instead of ashes, the oil of gladness instead of mourning, and a garment of praise instead of a spirit of despair. (NIV)

Many times rejection leads to desperation. But as the passage says, God is always there to comfort us and mend our broken hearts. After we realize that God has brought us hope and joy and we are released from the negative desperation that rejection has brought, we can begin to see the positive results of rejection.

One day at Velo, the girls prayed for me. We talked about the rejection each of us has faced in our lives. Then something clicked in my mind. I realized how powerful and anointed this group of girls truly is and how God uses them on a daily basis. Yet they are all so humble. I truly believe that if the other women had not had to face rejection, they would not be so humble.

Rejection, therefore, allows room for God to change us and bring humility to our lives. This allows God to use us in ways that would not be possible if we are not humble. This is the positive in rejection, the reason that rejection is worth fighting through. This allows us to know that no matter how badly we hurt, God uses the situation to make room for his will and purpose in our lives, and he will always strengthen us through the process of rejection.

> The Lord is good and does what is right; he shows the proper path to those who go astray. He leads the humble in doing right, teaching them his way.
> (Psalms 25:8–9, NLT)

What say you?

- Have you ever experienced rejection?
- Looking back, has rejection humbled you?
- Have you ever rejected another person?

EPISODE 18

It's Not Fair! *by Kristie K. McCrary*

"It's not fair!" We've all said that phrase at some point in our lives—probably to one or both of our parents. Maybe we said it the time our dad attempted to dismiss our whining about some potential emotional scarring or intense trauma we thought we were experiencing at the time. It might have been about the bullying of one of our siblings. Or perhaps our outburst of emotion came from having our request declined to spend the night with a friend our parents didn't approve of. Whatever the situation, most of the time, one or both of our parents emphatically replied, "Life's not fair. It's not fair now, and it never will be, so it would be in your best interest to accept it and stop complaining."

Well, they were right. Life really isn't fair. I believe "It's not fair" is a phrase we often find ourselves saying when we're at a loss for words or can't seem to be able to offer up a more comforting explanation. Somehow we convince ourselves that we are alone against the whole world, and we believe that we're the only people on the planet who ever experienced such an undesirable fate.

Life's not always going to be fair. If we allow ourselves to dwell on the past, we will never really move forward and be emotionally healthy. It's of utmost importance that we deal with whatever might be holding us as a prisoner and sincerely commit to moving forward.

Rather than complain, I think we should count our blessings. Was it fair for God to send his son, Jesus, to earth to die for us? Why did Jesus have to leave Heaven to come to an earth to die for us? Jesus knew before arriving on the earth to carry out his mission that we would never be able to repay the debt and price of his life. Yet there's not one time that he complained or replied to his father, "It's not fair!"

When you think about it, eternal life's not fair. Eternal life is a gift that can't be repaid or earned. It's given to us by the grace of Jesus Christ, because no one will enter Heaven's gates on the merit of living a good life and trying to do the right thing. Grace alone will get us to Heaven. Life will never be fair. However, if we concentrate on the goodness and grace of Jesus Christ, we can overcome anything we have to face.

> Have I not commanded you? Be strong and courageous. Do not be terrified; do not be discouraged, for the Lord your God will be with you wherever you go.
> (Joshua 1:9, NIV)

What say you?

- Are you carrying bitterness that comes from your past?
- Do you have an "it's not fair" mentality?
- Do you recognize the blessings in your life?

EPISODE 19

Distractions *by Melissa LaGrone*

The disciples witness Jesus feeding thousands of people with only a small amount of food. After the disciples collected the leftovers, Jesus, knowing that they needed to cross a body of water, told the disciples to leave without him. Perhaps he wanted to pray by himself, but I also think that Jesus knew what was about to happen. When he went to find the disciples, the boat had already sailed a considerable distance from shore, so Jesus walked on the water to catch up. Peter saw him and began to walk to Jesus. Except when Peter got halfway to his Lord, the wind distracted him. Peter got scared and started to sink.

I have read that passage many times and heard many sermons using that text. Those sermons have always focused on Peter's lack of faith and how the act of taking his eyes off of Jesus caused him to sink. After reading this passage again, what sticks out most in my mind is not Peter's lack of faith, but the cause of his lack of faith. Peter didn't take his eyes off of Jesus until he became distracted.

Christians today have the same struggle as Peter had many years ago. They want to trust God, and they even ask him to tell them what to do with their lives. Most of us are very sincere with our requests and really want to know God's will for our lives. We start out great, and we think we know what is going on. As long as we are on a clear path and can see what he is doing and where he is taking us, we do fine. But the minute things don't go our way—life takes a turn, the path gets clouded, or God tells us to do something we don't understand—we begin to doubt. We don't doubt because we don't trust God; we doubt because things around us distract us, and those distractions cause fear.

When things that we don't understand and can't explain begin to happen in our lives, we usually get scared and cry out for help from God, thinking that he has left us. We forget that God hasn't left us, we just haven't trusted him to take care of the situation. The Bible tells us, in 2 Timothy 1:7 "For God has not given us a spirit of fear, but of power and of love and of a sound mind" (NKJV). God never intended for us to be afraid, which is why so many preachers talk about keeping our eyes on Jesus. Only when we focus on other things, such as fear, do we allow ourselves to be distracted.

So I encourage you not to let distractions, like fear, cause you to take your eyes off of Jesus. He is with you. He has your best interests in mind in every situation. Don't let fear distract you from the path that God has placed you on. Trust him and know that when things don't seem to go the way you think they should, God may be using the situation to see if you will trust him and let him lead you or let the distractions of life cause you to take your eyes off of him and sink.

> In righteousness you will be established: Tyranny will be far from you; you will have nothing to fear. Terror will be far removed; it will not come near you.
> (Isaiah 54:14, NIV)

What say you?

- Are there any distractions in your life that could possibly be distracting from Jesus and his will for your life?
- Could fear be causing you to doubt God?

EPISODE 20
Something Doesn't Quite Fit Right (Element 1) *by Baileigh Robertson*

Have you ever tried to squeeze into a pair of jeans that used to fit you well, but all of a sudden, they just don't? Let me just tell you that there's a lot I try to succeed at in life, and I must admit that slipping easily into my favorite pair of jeans is on that list. Sit down for a minute, put your feet up, and let me tell a heart-wrenching tale of struggle and defeat.

One day during the spring semester of my freshmen year of college I found myself in quite a rush. I had just gotten out late from my last class, thanks to a long-winded professor. I couldn't grab lunch, and I had just enough time to grab my work clothes out of the dryer at my dorm, change my clothes, and hurry off to my part-time job. Well, really I had twenty minutes, and that was pushing it.

I made it back to my dorm with seventeen minutes on the clock. I attempted to put on my favorite jeans. Something awful had happened. My jeans didn't fit! I proceeded to suck in and tug and pull and hold my breath until I urged myself to stop and think through what must have happened. The drier's temperature must have broken, and I must have used too much heat; thus, my pants shrunk. Well, if that wasn't it, maybe someone else's jeans had ended up in my clothes because so many students used the driers, and I, being in a rush, hadn't noticed and had put on someone else's jeans. The only other thing that could possibly be the reason for this misfortune was....

Wait—eleven minutes on the clock! I was going to be late for sure. As I opted for something else to wear, I decided to stop making myself feel better with excuses and face the music. Was I having my first encounter with the dreaded myth of the "Freshmen Fifteen"? I hopped on the scale in my bathroom to find that the myth I had heard my upper classmen friends rant about had finally found its way to my hips.

Sometime since then that story sparked a thought in me; let me share it. I think you can agree with me that there's not much else more depressing than not fitting into your clothes. So what do we do? We work out. We get up early in the morning to make our bodies fit. We watch what we eat and supplement our diet appropriately. We talk with our friends about what has worked for them, and we subscribe to magazines to help us stay abreast of the latest and best tips to keep us lean and trim. We use motivational mottos and personal trainers to make sure we are doing all we can to keep ourselves looking good: our muscles toned and our figures lean.

I wonder, though, with all that we do to make sure that we look good on the outside, do we spend the necessary amount of time to make sure we look good on the inside? What I'm really getting at is do we spend as much time working on our heart as we do our hips. Do we think as much about our godly character as we do about our dress size?

Well, that's a tough question because I know that if we were really honest, the answer to that question might very well be no. I know that there have been times when I have been more dedicated to my workout than to my daily Bible reading. There have been instances when prayer has not seemed as urgent, and worship seemed to be more of an extracurricular activity than a means of connection with my Savior, Jesus. That should not be the case. If something is off track on the inside, it doesn't matter how much tweaking we do on the outside. We still need daily rejuvenation from the lover of our hearts and souls. Listen to the wisdom God's word offers:

> Charm is deceptive, and beauty is fleeting; but a woman who fears the Lord is to be praised.
> (Proverbs 31:30, NIV) b

What say you?

- Do you think more about what you look like on the outside or what you look like on the inside?
- Do you have "spending time with God" on your daily schedule, or are you too busy?
- Is your relationship with God a priority?

EPISODE 21
Something Doesn't Quite Fit Right (Element 2) *by Baileigh Robertson*

Have you ever met any stubborn children? I know that's a funny question, but I feel like I can ask because I was a stubborn child. It's true! One time, I was putting a puzzle together with a little girl, who was very sweet and a lot like me when I was her age—good-hearted, but hard-headed. Anyway, I was trying to show her that a certain piece of the puzzle she was holding just wouldn't work.

"Yes, it will!" She insisted, "I know exactly what I'm doing, and I know it will fit this way—just … just … gimme a minute!" Needless to say, that puzzle piece didn't fit. As a matter of fact, my little friend pushed so hard, the rounded edge bent. It wasn't meant to go into that hole of the puzzle. It just didn't fit.

Have you ever seen people try to live life that way? Have you ever tried to live that way yourself? Has there ever been something you wanted to do or tried to do, but it just didn't seem like a good fit? I think we can all think of a time or two that we look back on and think, *Why did I ever try that? That wasn't me at all.* Or maybe we thought, *I really should be doing something else, but what?*

There is something about the very nature of that beast that makes me sad to my core. There's so much more out there for you than for your head to be filled with shouldas, couldas, and wouldas. The Bible talks about how God has given specific gifts and callings to each one of our lives.

> His divine power has given us everything we need for life and godliness through our knowledge of him who called us by his own glory and goodness. Through these he has given us his very great and precious promises, so that through them you may participate in the divine nature and escape the corruption in the world caused by evil desires.
>
> For this very reason, make every effort to add to your faith goodness; and to goodness, knowledge; and to knowledge, self-control; and to self-control, perseverance; and to perseverance, godliness; and

> to godliness, brotherly kindness; and to brotherly kindness, love. For if you possess these qualities in increasing measure, they will keep you from being ineffective and unproductive in your knowledge of our Lord Jesus Christ. But if anyone does not have them, he is nearsighted and blind, and has forgotten that he has been cleansed from his past sins.
> Therefore, my brothers, be all the more eager to make your calling and election sure. For if you do these things, you will never fall, and you will receive a rich welcome into the eternal kingdom of our Lord and Savior Jesus Christ. (2 Peter 1:3–11, NIV)

Keeping these things in the forefront of our minds as we shape our hearts will allow our walk with God to develop and keep us from being "ineffective and unproductive." I love that! You were meant to live in such a way as to find your fit. You are a very important piece of the puzzle in the beautiful picture of God's kingdom.

> Many women do noble things, but you surpass them all. (Proverbs 31:29, NIV)

What say you?

- Do you know your specific gifts or the unique call of God in your life?
- Do you ever pray and ask God to reveal your gifts to you and how you can use them for him?

EPISODE 22
To Be or to Do? That Is the Question *by Aunie Brooks*

When I was a little girl, I thought trophies were the coolest things. I always remember wishing I had more. I had a few from cheerleading events, from my church's missionettes program, and from piano recitals. But other than that I didn't have very many. I had a friend who played soccer and gymnastics. She had an entire dresser covered with trophies. I remember my mouth watering to have that many! I, along with many other American children, learned at a young age that you have to perform in order to be rewarded in life.

Life is about what you can do. Even as an adult, you are awarded for how well you perform your job. Better work, better money. How come we can't get raises just for becoming a better person? I think that if God had his way, that's exactly what would happen. The more I read scripture and spend time in prayer, the more I realize that God is more concerned with who I become than what I do. What a freeing thought.

Yet at the same time, it's a thought that I have a hard time grasping. After all, since I was a child, the world has been screaming a different message at me. I have spent hours—no, years—stressing over what I'm going to do with my life. What job will I have? What education should I get? Where will I live? What will my ministry in the church be? And the list goes on.

Each time I have these questions, I do what any respectable Christian would do. I take it to the Lord in prayer. I ask God, "What do you want me to do?" Every time, his response is, "Love the Lord your God with all your heart and with all your soul and with all your strength and with all your mind. And love your neighbor as yourself" (Luke 10:27, NIV). And my response is always, "Okay, God, but how do you want me to do that? Do you want me to teach, write, be a missionary?" I think he just smiles and thinks, "Eventually, she'll get it."

Look at Jesus. He was a carpenter. Really, God, that's the plan you had for your only son? Jesus had the most important calling in history, and he spent his days working as a carpenter? That's not what stood out about Christ. Who he was stood out. He was sinless. He was holy and pure. He was love, is love, and will forever be love. God is the great I AM, and that's what makes us admire him. Sure, Jesus performed the greatest action mankind has ever heard about: he died on the cross for our salvation. But the only reason there's power in that action is because of who he is. He is sinless, the Son of God. Only he can save us through his sacrifice.

Paul got it. In Philippians 3:7, 10–11, he says:

> Whatever was to my profit I now consider loss for the sake of Christ... I want to know Christ and the power of his resurrection and the fellowship of sharing in his sufferings, becoming like him in his death, and so, somehow, to attain to the resurrection from the dead. (NIV)

All those trophies and awards—whatever was to my profit I now consider loss.

Nothing compares to knowing Christ and becoming like him. When we focus on who we become more than on what we do, then what we do will fall into place, and it will be anointed because of who we are.

> I consider everything a loss compared to the surpassing greatness of knowing Christ Jesus my Lord, for whose sake I have lost all things. I consider them rubbish, that I may gain Christ and be found in him, not having a righteousness of my own that comes from the law, but that which is through faith in Christ—the righteousness that comes from God and is by faith.
> (Philippians3:8–9, NIV)

What say you?

- Ask yourself, "What am I going to do? Who am I going to be?"
- Do you strive to know who God is?

EPISODE 23
Mac Daddy, Fix It! *by Kristie K. McCrary*

Have you ever thought about the way you open your conversations with God?

If I'm not careful, at times, I catch myself settling into a "Mac Daddy, fix it" rant rather than an actual dialogue with the Lord—"I need this, I want that, this is a problem, I'm feeling this way or that way, and yada, yada, yada." Often I have to remind myself to get past that phase and just praise the Lord for who he is. Then I praise him for his loving nature, which is merciful and eternal.

In Psalm 136, David wrote about the love of God, and that thought repeats continually throughout the psalm. David went beyond thanking the Lord for creating the moon and the stars and became completely wrapped up in the almighty God, focusing on his nature rather than what he is actually doing at that time. David is basically saying, "God, you love me unconditionally, and your love is forever. It will never change," rather than "God, you didn't give me this, and you didn't give me that, and I need your help now."

David knew that he had been anointed to be the next king of Israel in his early teens, and he had lived with and served King Saul as a loyal protégé. But when he wrote Psalm 136, he found himself hiding in the desert and caves for twelve and a half years, after Saul tried to murder him on several occasions.

So how did David become so infectiously thankful to the Lord that he repeats, "Your love endures forever"? How did he find the resilience to praise God about some incredibly difficult circumstances? He found peace to praise God by being entirely wrapped up in the love and nature of God, rather than in his current and past circumstances.

When I'm faced with a difficult situation, and things seem to be going in the wrong direction, I have learned to get into the word of God and stay in it. No matter what the circumstance, I position myself to live under the manifestation of God's love in a very real and personal way, just as David did.

When I stay in the word and concentrate on God's love for me, I find that confusion cannot conquer the theater of my mind, because I am focused on who God is rather than what he can do for me.

Remember the words and thoughts of David. He is correct—God's love endures forever.

> Give thanks to the Lord, for he is good. His love endures forever.
> (Psalm 136:1, NIV)

What say you?

- Do you praise and thank God for all the things he has already done for you?
- Do you ever have times that you just love God and praise him for who he is?
- What is the focus of your prayer time with God? Are your prayers balanced with prayer requests and praise to Him, or are they constantly centered on what God can do for you?

EPISODE 24
Just Praise *by Melisa Conner*

The word tribulation was derived from a word meaning "thresh." Threshing evokes a rather violent image in my mind—a painful twisting from the inside to the outside. God always does everything intentionally. Please exercise your faith muscles with me for a minute and believe that God has a plan and a reason for every trial, testing, and threshing that we are allowed to walk through.

I fought and wrestled for the peace of God, which he speaks of in his word: And God's peace [shall be yours, that tranquil state of a soul assured of its salvation through Christ, and so fearing nothing from God and being content with its earthly lot of whatever sort that is, that peace] which transcends all understanding shall garrison and mount guard over your hearts and minds in Christ Jesus" (Philippians 4:7, AB). Hallelujah! Peace is ours for the asking. It is a gift from God, and one we don't have to fight or strive to attain. We do have to decide, however, to *receive* it from him.

We can't become stronger, wiser, or more resilient without going through certain experiences.

> Moreover [let us also be full of joy now!] let us exult and triumph in our troubles and rejoice in our sufferings, knowing that pressure and affliction and hardship produce patient and unswerving endurance.
>
> And endurance (fortitude) develops maturity of character (approved faith and tried integrity). And character [of this sort] produces [the habit of] joyful and confident hope of eternal salvation. (Romans 5:3–4, AB)

Notice that God didn't say we should exult and triumph *for* our troubles; he said we should exult *in* our troubles. This doesn't mean we should be happy about the struggle but that we should find ways to triumph despite that struggle.

Sometimes it is hard to find God while we experience physical and emotional pain.

My sister, Paige, taught me to get really honest, even raw, with him. He knows all of our thoughts, so it would be a waste of time not to come to him with our deepest hurts, our disappointments, and even our anger. This is an integral part of real intimacy, which frees us from holding these toxic emotions inside. Honesty with God allows us to then praise and exult in him, even when we are tired, hurting, discouraged, and worn out. We must decide to praise him and fix our eyes on Jesus, who is our high priest (Hebrews 4:15, AB), and not on our circumstances, our pain, our stress, our financial troubles, etc.

During the past several months, there have been times when I have become discouraged, defeated, and depressed, giving in to the way I felt. I decided to praise God for his goodness anyway, and it helped me get to a new place. I told a friend, "It's like God has me in a sort of spiritual boot camp." I decided that God had something for me to learn. I trust that I will come away with pearls of wisdom. It really is an exchange—you pray for strength and wisdom, and God answers that prayer with life experience.

> Fear not [there is nothing to fear], for I am with you;
> do not look around you in terror and be dismayed,
> for I am your God. I will strengthen and harden you
> to difficulties, yes, I will help you; yes, I will hold you
> up and retain you with My [victorious] right hand of
> rightness and justice. (Isaiah 41:10, AB)

One of my friends recently made a statement that made a real impact on me—"Girls, weak is the new strong." If we will just let ourselves collapse in his arms, and truly need him, he will never abandon us.

Children of the Most High God, always remember that God—who is love; who is the most powerful force in existence—loves you. He asks that we trust him. He knows that we will never rise above our circumstances by relying on our own strength and ability. Nor will we take our eyes off of our own pain long enough to have the kind of faith we need to praise him for his goodness. You will experience a breakthrough when you praise God during the difficult times. God is faithful. I pray that God's grace will be so strong in your life that you will begin to really get it. I pray that you will understand how much he really loves you, cherishes you, and values you.

God wants us to be joyful. He doesn't want us to live defeated, discouraged lives. Trust in the Lord, and commit all of your ways to him. He will never let you down, and you will be blessed.

> Let everything that has breath praise the Lord. Praise the Lord. (Psalm 150:6, NIV)

What say you?

- Do you rejoice and praise God in the midst of trials?
- Have past trials and experiences made you stronger and wiser? Or have they made you bitter and fearful?

EPISODE 25

Palm Trees *by Suzette Perlmutter*

One of the greatest of life's lessons is one I learned from a palm tree. That may sound crazy, but it's true. I came across some information stating that when a palm tree is measured the day after a hurricane, it can have grown up to an inch. This made me stop and think. The hurricane winds can reach high velocities of over a hundred miles per hour, and yet the palm tree digs its roots deep and hangs on. When the storm quiets, the tree not only still stands, but also it has grown up to an inch.

We Christians could learn from that. God allows certain storms and problems to come our way. I know we sometimes ask God, "Why?" and "How could you let this happen?" But God works it out not only for good, but also to the greater overall benefit for each of us as individuals.

As we persevere through life's most painful times and situations, there is a day when the sun comes out again. Then we realize that the tears have stopped, the pain has left, and not only are we okay, but also we can physically feel the strength God has given us. We aren't the same people we once were. We are better people because of the pain. The very situation we thought was our torment was actually an unforeseen opportunity to see God turn tragedy to victory.

There is life after pain—not just an ordinary life, but a life to live knowing what it's like to need and receive comfort. Now we, being a stronger person, can comfort someone else. That, which doesn't kill us, makes us stronger. We should all take a lesson from the palm tree. When the storms of life come to take us over, we must dig in and stand strong. You will not only make it through, but you will be that much closer to the woman or man of God that he is shaping you to be.

> And the God of all grace, who called you to his eternal glory in Christ, after you have suffered a little while, will himself restore you and make you strong, firm and steadfast.
> (1 Peter 5:10, NIV)

What say you?

- What do you tend to do and how do you typically react during personal storms?
- Looking back on your last personal storm, did it make you stronger or weaken you?

EPISODE 26

Passion Principle *by Kristie K. McCrary*

The Old Testament is full of stories about true principles that we often learned as children. As we've gotten older, we've forgotten these stories or pushed them aside. We rarely revisit their principles and retain the value of their messages, yet at times, we need to dust off the shelf of childhood memories and refresh the muted colors of the past.

The third chapter of the book of Daniel recounts the true story of three young, Hebrew men who faced a challenge to prove the certainty of their beliefs.

Under the leadership of King Nebuchadnezzar, Shadrach, Meshach, and Abednego found themselves eating and drinking differently and even answering to different names as they strived to survive in a world that threatened their identities.

Jerusalem had surrendered to Babylonian control and King Nebuchadnezzar had ordered the building of a ninety foot golden statue. The day of the unveiling of the golden statue arrived, along with all of the pomp and circumstance a powerful king could provide. King Nebuchadnezzar decreed, "Anyone who does not kneel and worship shall be thrown immediately into a roaring furnace" (Daniel 3:6, MSG).

As the people began to bow to the idol, Shadrach, Meshach, and Abednego remained upright and tall, void of even a squirm. The king received word that they had not bowed to his idol, and Nebuchadnezzar gave the trio a second chance. However, the chance came with a hearty warning that went something like this: "Guys, if you refuse to bow to the idol a second time, I will usurp my power and throw all of you immediately into the toasty blaze."

Without a flinch, Shadrach, Meshach, and Abednego answered King Nebuchadnezzar,

> Your threat means nothing to us. If you throw us in the fire, the God we serve can rescue us from your roaring furnace and anything else you might cook up, O king. But even if he doesn't, it wouldn't make a bit of difference, O king. We still wouldn't serve your

> gods or worship the gold statue you set up. (Daniel 3:16–18, MSG)

Shadrach, Meshach, and Abednego refused, based on principle, to bow to a golden idol. I call it the passion principle because, without passion, these guys could never have withstood the consequences or the pressure of their decision.

Without sincere passion and belief in their God, as strong as these three lads seemed to be, they could never have withstood the pressures of that dramatic experience. Passion for their God and a certainty of their beliefs were required in order to have made the right, but very difficult and costly, decision that day.

They stood on their principles. They said simply something like this, "We may be in Babylon but our hearts are in Jerusalem and under the Jewish law and belief system." Their religious beliefs were coupled with character and the passion principle. That's why they became strong during adversity and were not willing to surrender their souls.

Today we may not be living in Babylon, yet we do live in a culture that constantly impedes our religious beliefs, questioning us for who and what we are every single day. Will we be like Shadrach, Meshach, and Abednego and stand tall when we're confronted with temptation and compromise? The Christian community is searching desperately for the Shadrachs, Meshachs, and Abednegos of our generation. In order to step into the shoes of these courageous young men, it will require a counterculture movement that will take tremendous regard for principle. It will take the passion principle.

> We preach Christ, warning people not to add to the Message. We teach in a spirit of profound common sense so that we can bring each person to maturity. To be mature is to be basic. Christ! No more, no less. That's what I'm working so hard at day after day, year after year, doing my best with the energy God so generously gives me.
> (Colossians 1:28–29, MSG)

What say you?

- How do you handle the temptations of the world? Do you tend to compromise?

- Do you know what you believe and what the Word of God really says?
- Do you live the "passion principle"?

EPISODE 27
Unconditionally *by Kim Yarbrough*

Unfortunately, we've all experienced the pain of disappointing relationships. Best friends grow cold; a couple finds itself facing a divorce; neighbors stop speaking; churches split over a divided opinion; relatives become enemies. I believe we might have forgotten about forgiveness.

Repairing a damaged relationship is extremely hard, but definitely not impossible. When we look to Jesus Christ as our example, we can see the steps we need to take to make peace. After all, 1 John 4:9–10 says that if God himself who made the first move to reunite us with Him. Even while we were still sinners and separated from God, He made the first move to prove His love for us. "This is how God showed his love among us: He sent his one and only Son into the world that we might live through him. This is love: not that we loved God, but that he loved us and sent his Son as an atoning sacrifice for our sins" (NIV). That's what I call taking the first step toward reconciliation.

How do we model Christ's love? How do we follow the example of our Heavenly Father and choose to love the unloving? How do we forgive and love others unconditionally even when we were their innocent victims? We must be one hundred percent dependent on the Holy Spirit to be our comforter, our guide, and our counselor. In our human strength, there is no possibility of loving or forgiving. Jesus said, "But I say to you who hear: Love your enemies, do good to those who hate you, bless those who curse you, and pray for those who spitefully use you" (Luke 6:27–28, NKJV).

I know what you are thinking: "Kim, you just don't know what I've been through. I have a right to be mad." Well, you probably do. However, Christ said to forgive someone seventy times seven times.

Unforgiveness helps you to feel justified for a season. But you've got to be careful not to give the enemy a foothold into your mind. Reject those thoughts that stem from pride and disobedience to God's word. Of course, you have a right to be mad or hurt, but we must also have the right attitude toward those who have offended and harmed us.

We live in a culture that opposes God's word and can't fathom what true love and forgiveness are all about—"Forgiving each other, just as in Christ God forgave you" (Ephesians 4:32, NIV). We must make a decision to practice unconditional love. It's easy to model the world, but are we ready to model Christ? The next time someone offends or disappoints you, try to think about Philippians 4:8: "Finally, brothers, whatever is true, whatever is noble, whatever is right, whatever is pure, whatever is lovely, whatever is admirable—if anything is excellent or praiseworthy—think about such things" (NIV).

Forgiveness is never easy, but it's incredibly rewarding and comes with overwhelming freedom. Augustine said, "If you are suffering from a bad man's injustice, forgive him lest there be two bad men." I believe Augustine had it right! It's always better to forgive and love your offender unconditionally.

> But I tell you, Do not resist an evil person. If someone strikes you on the right cheek, turn to him the other also.
> (Matthew 5:39, NIV)

What say you?

- Is there a relationship in your life that needs to be repaired?
- Do you have a difficult time forgiving others or accepting forgiveness?
- Do you believe that unconditional love is realistic and possible?

EPISODE 28
Is Your Love Worth Giving? *by Marla D. Monreal*

What comes to mind when I say the word "love"? Do you think of family, friends, or spouses? Do you think of perfect couples, or is your mind consumed with the idea of perfect love?

I have heard so many sermons telling me to love as Christ did. That may sound too far out of reach for our human nature. You may think *I cannot love like that.* You may say, "I get easily irritated" or "I have a short temper" or, simply, "I do not even like everyone around me." God can enable us to love as he did. God can fill us with his love and allow that love to flow through us. The more we grow in love with God, the more we will be able to share his love with everyone we may come in contact with.

Ephesians 5:2 says, "Mostly what God does is love you. Keep company with him and learn a life of love. Observe how Christ loved us. His love was not cautious but extravagant. He didn't love in order to get something from us but to give everything of himself to us. Love like that" (MSG). In order to learn to love like Christ, we have to truly know him and be in company with him. He is ready and willing to give of himself so that we might share who he is with others. God's love is selfless. We should love, not looking for something in return, but just as a gift that flows through us from Christ.

Living a life of love does not just include words. I believe that, so many times, we are selective in who we choose to share Christ's' love with. We must share his love by who we are on a daily basis. You can share God's love with everyone you come in contact with. Small things make all the difference in the world.

We can learn to share his love by changing our mind-sets. We need to see the value of every person whom we come in contact with on a daily basis. Sometimes we may see people as less then ourselves, but every single person has value in the eyes of God. God created each person with a purpose. Seeing every person as someone valued and cherished by God can be the first step to sharing his love. In today's society, time is a valued gift. We should take the time to encourage someone, smile at someone, or simply remember how we would want to be treated. Our actions can portray the love of Christ. We must learn to see people through the eyes of God and not through our own eyes.

Sometimes we are too busy to acknowledge the people God places in our paths. We miss opportunities to make a difference and allow someone to feel loved and valued. Every person has unsurpassed worth in the eyes of Christ. God's love can only flow through us if we allow room in our hearts, lives, and who we are for him to come and fill us.

Whatever feeling and emotions we allow into our lives is what we will share with those around us. Make a conscious choice to love as Christ did. So many times we feel inadequate when it comes to sharing Christ. God has given each and every one of us the ability to love. He designed your personality and who you are. Use the gifts that God has given you to be a blessing to others and share Christ's love with everyone you encounter. Is your love worth giving?

> "So this is my prayer: that your love will flourish and that you will not only love much but well. Learn to love appropriately. You need to use your head and test your feelings so that your love is sincere and intelligent, not sentimental gush. Live a lover's life, circumspect and exemplary, a life Jesus will be proud of: bountiful in fruits from the soul, making Jesus Christ attractive to all, getting everyone involved in the glory and praise of God."
> (Philippians 1:9–11, MSG)

What say you?

- Do you take the time to love others?
- What are some specific ways that you can show love to others?
- Do you treat others the way you would like to be treated?

EPISODE 29
Sweet Sanity *by Khia Paige*

A special fulfillment is associated with serving in missions. It is a joy to help children grow in wisdom, stature, and favor with God and man (Luke 2:52). In life there are mountaintop experiences and valleys. The period I want to tell you about was the granddaddy of all valley experiences. Mistakenly, I began to let the season dictate my emotions.

A certain man, who we nicknamed Abe, lived in the same building as the missionaries when I served in Korea. Abe was crude; he reeked of sweat, alcohol, cigarettes, and the trash he went through looking for food. Our hearts went out to him, because his addictions put him in bondage, leaving him impoverished and starving. After seeing him rummage through the trash time after time, we contemplated making him a home-cooked meal. In the end, we decided the act would be like giving milk to a stray cat. What Abe needed was deliverance. We all diligently prayed for deliverance. One of the missionaries, Liz, really wanted to see the demonic oppression lifted, and she prayed intensely for Abe.

We often saw Abe laughing, talking, and sometimes fighting with invisible friends. Abe hated noise of any type, unless he was the one making it. When anyone made too much clatter or laughed too loudly, Abe fumed, and smoke blew out of his ears. On many days he expressed his irritation at us by screaming as loudly as he could in Korean. Abe was explicit about his demands; he wanted us to come into the building, tiptoe upstairs, go to our rooms, quietly close the doors, and remain silent. He didn't need joyful missionaries making his hangovers worse than they already were.

One day we did not honor Abe's demands and he had a fit. Abe had had enough. Who did we think we were? Abe came out of his room, yelled in Korean, went back inside, and then came out with a big butcher knife! At that point, we fled five separate ways. Abe decided to follow Liz. I just knew my pounding heart would explode. In my room I cried and trembled, fearing this might be my last missionary opportunity. Would I be next? God was faithful in protecting us. Liz walked away from the threat physically unharmed, though emotionally and psychologically shaken.

The incident reinforced and magnified my discouragement. For the first time in my life, I felt like I might go crazy. The purpose of the attack was twofold: to install fear in all of our hearts, and for Liz to give up her burden for Abe. In contrast, God caused this occurrence to deepen our intercession for Abe. God erased all fear and replaced it with boldness. I knew giving up was not an option. In unity, we stood on James 5:16, which says that "the prayer of a righteous man is powerful and effective" (NIV). My spirit was damaged and broken, but sweet Jesus is the restorer of all broken things.

When the enemy comes to captivate your thoughts, tell him he can't have them. According to Isaiah 26:3, God will give us perfect peace when we keep our mind on him. In the past, I have been grateful to God for his faithfulness and for the doors he has opened. I am blessed to have walked away from that season in my life with my sanity intact. Yes, you heard right, I consider having a sane mind a blessing. I am sane, praise God! God has been the mender of my broken heart and the lifter of my head.

> And all your [spiritual] children shall be disciples [taught by the Lord and obedient to His will], and great shall be the peace and undisturbed composure of your children.
> (Isaiah 54:13, AMP)

What say you?

- Is there a situation or person that causes you to experience fear?
- How do you face your personal fears?
- Do you believe in the promises of God, which allow you the opportunity to activate your faith and live a life of peace?

EPISODE 30
They Are His *by Missy Lares*

Have you ever come to a point in life when you just feel like giving up on people? There are loved ones in my life who I truly love and really care for. They say they're going to change. They say they want more of God in their lives, but their actions speak louder than their words. I watch all the distractions and excuses and wonder if today will be their day? I think to myself, *when will they give it all to God? When will enough be enough? When will they allow God control of their hearts?* At times, it's scary to see our loved ones not living for Christ or doing what they know is right. We watch them go through the consequences of sin and hope that, one day, they will get it right.

Well, I'm glad God has not given up on us. His love, mercy, and grace extend to us, even when we have turned our backs on him. Christ's death on the cross allowed all of these blessings to be possible. He knows exactly what we need and when we need it. Our job as Christians is to love people. God does not tell us to love conditionally; he told us to love just as Christ loved us.

Sometimes, when I think it may be too late for some people, God reminds me of Lazarus whom Christ raised him from the dead in John 11. Mary and Martha were brokenhearted that Jesus had not come back to Judea in time to heal Lazarus from his illness. God's timing is never off. It's perfect. Mary and Martha thought their brother was dead, but Jesus said "Our friend Lazarus has fallen asleep; but I am going there to wake him up" (John 11:11, NIV). In the meantime, Jesus was a great example of what we need to do when waiting: pray. "Father, I thank you that you have heard me. I knew that you always hear me, but I said this for the benefit of the people standing here, that they may believe that you sent me" (John 11:41, NIV).

Jesus knows our pain when our loved ones don't surrender to Christ right away. He also weeps with us. Just like Mary and Martha, who thought their brother was dead and there was no time left, were heartbroken over their loss. Christ was at work, and at the perfect time, he called "Lazarus, come out" (John 11:43, NIV). It was a miracle. Lazarus was raised from the dead. Similarly our loved ones are spiritually dead, the Holy Spirit calls to them and will prove God to be great through their weakness.

We need to trust God with the people we love the most. He has not forgotten about our lost loved ones. They are like that one sheep that was lost and the most important to the shepherd. We need to trust, pray, and believe that God will do what he says he will do. And most of all, we need to just love them because they are his.

> For my thoughts are not your thoughts, neither are your ways my ways," declares the Lord. "As the heavens are higher than the earth, so are my ways higher than your ways and my thoughts than your thoughts.
> (Isaiah 55:8–9, NIV)

What say you?

- Do you have a loved one, or someone close to you, who does not know the salvation of the Lord?
- Are you praying for them regularly and trusting that God will bring them back to him?
- Do you believe God can work a miracle in your family?

EPISODE 31
Love Them Anyway *by Aunie Brooks*

Sometimes life doesn't turn out the way you think it will or even should; still, don't stop living or giving all that you have to give. I recently heard a popular song with this message in it and every time I hear it I literally get goose bumps. No matter how much you love someone, they can still choose to walk away. Just accept the risk and love them anyway.

I think the reason this rests so powerfully with me right now is because about a year ago my husband and I faced one of the most important decisions any young married couple faces: "Are we ready for children?" I can remember battling between the maternal emotions of longing to cradle a little person in my arms each night and the knowledge of the sacrifice it costs parents to bring a child into the world. After many discussions and moments of prayer, we decided we were ready. As I write this, I am thirteen weeks pregnant, and I couldn't be more ecstatic.

No matter how excited I am about this new life that's on its way, thankfulness is not my only emotion. Almost immediately after the joy comes fear—fear, fear, and more fear. What if I'm not a good mom? What if we make terrible mistakes as parents and ruin our child's life? Or worse. What if we're perfect parents? What if we do all we can to raise our child well and he/she still chooses to walk away from God? My husband and I work full-time in the ministry and I've seen plenty of pastors' kids who have rebelled wildly and hurt their parents in so many ways. What if that were to happen to us?

As I spiraled downward in my fear, the Lord used this opportunity to teach me something extremely humbling. He reminded me that he knows all things. This means that when he created men and women, he knew what that meant ahead of time. He knew that there would be plenty who would turn their backs on him and lead lives that insulted him. He knew that he would be embarrassed and angered, but most of all hurt and betrayed. Yet, he created us anyway. Because he also knew that while some would choose death, many would choose life. And as a Father, nothing brings more joy than to watch your children choose to love you and serve you and live with you. To him, it was worth the risk.

This truth has been so comforting to me. It's risky to bring a child into this world. It's risky to pour your life into loving someone more than you love yourself. It's risky to put someone else's desires and needs above your own for eighteen or more years of your life. And the whole time, you know that at any point they can choose to walk away. I want my love to be as risky as God's love. I want to love them anyway.

> Do nothing out of selfish ambition or vain conceit, but in humility consider others better than yourselves. Each of you should look not only to your own interests, but also to the interests of others. Your attitude should be the same as that of Christ Jesus.
> (Philippians 2:3–5, NIV)

What say you?

- Are you willing to take a risk and just love people?
- Are you afraid of being hurt or disappointed in a relationship?

EPISODE 32

Risky Business *by Kristie K. McCrary*

The people you spend time with will determine your level out of the box. If you want to be a dreamer, you need to hang out with people who encourage your dreams. If you are a couch potato, you should spend your quality time with fellow couch potatoes. If you're serious about your walk with the Lord and want to make a significant impact in your world, you need to develop quality relationships with other believers. It's a simple fact of life that's been passed down from generation to generation and from century to century.

In today's world so many things that were unacceptable to our parents and grandparents are now acceptable. Our generation and culture has become lackadaisical in our fundamental principles and values, positioning us in a very precarious situation. We can walk into any church today and not really know who's genuine and who's not. I remember that when I was growing up, if I hadn't been on my best behavior over the course of the week, I dreaded walking through the church doors on Sunday. The guilt of not living up to God's laws and my potential weighed heavily on my heart as I sat quietly, hoping that the pastor, special speaker, or some god-fearing elderly lady within the church walls wouldn't call me out and expose my spiritual insincerity. Every time I found myself in that situation it was emotional torture. It blows my mind the way things have changed.

Members of our generation can live their lives any way they wish during the week, knowing full well what's right and what's wrong, enter the church property on Sunday, possibly even assume some position of leadership, and not even flinch. There's little, if any, awareness of the consequences of sin. We have become numb and rebellious, maintaining a disregard for the laws of God.

It dawned on me one day. Risky relationships aren't just found outside of the church walls, they're everywhere we go, including inside our comfort zone in today's Christian generation. Jude warned us of this as he addressed the Christian community:

> Dear friends, I've dropped everything to write you about this life of salvation that we have in common. I have to write insisting—begging! —that you fight

> with everything you have in you for this faith entrusted to us as a gift to guard and cherish. What has happened is that some people have infiltrated our ranks (our Scriptures warned us this would happen), who beneath their pious skin are shameless scoundrels. Their design is to replace the sheer grace of our God with sheer license—which means doing away with Jesus Christ, our one and only Master.
> (Jude 1:3–4, MSG)

By not taking the law of God seriously, our generation is volunteering itself to enter into risky business. Don't misunderstand me. I'm not writing this to be self-righteous. I'm simply relating the facts as I see them as a member of today's culture. There are people and situations that manipulate you before you realize it. I understand that it's a fine line. However, it's reality.

I'm not of the opinion that to live a pure and holy life before God you have to give up everything that's enjoyable and become some kind of freak. I know that we have to be relevant. We just have to find a way to balance it with holiness. How do you know if holiness has kicked in? It's simple. Holiness does not mean being able to properly check off the Christian dos-and-don'ts list. That's not enough. Holiness exists when the opportunities of the world present themselves, and they don't appeal to you any longer. That's when you know that you have genuinely embraced holiness and you're on a healthy track.

Be careful about who you choose as your close friends, and surround yourself with people who will help you make things happen in a positive way. Stay away from the wrong relationships. They're risky business and not worth the consequences.

> Keep a firm grasp on both your character and your teaching. Don't be diverted. Just keep at it. Both you and those who hear you will experience salvation.
> (1 Timothy 4.16, MSG)

What say you?

- Are you taking advantage of the forgiveness and grace of God?

- Are you striving to live a pure life, or are you involved in "risky business?"
- What type of friends do you surround yourself with? Are they positive, healthy, and pure?

EPISODE 33

Gossip *by Priscilla Van Winkle*

I want to talk about a power tool that you can't find at any hardware store. There's not enough money in the world to buy it, but yet it is the most popular and used piece of equipment out there. Believe it or not, this power tool comes easy for ladies to use, but men typically have to search for a manual just to shut it off. What is it? It is the mouth of a woman.

As women, one of the hardest battles is fought against gossip. We can't even go to the bathroom alone—we take a fleet of bloodthirsty gossiping queens and travel like a pack of wolves ready to devour its prey.

I would be lying if I said I didn't struggle with gossip myself. Occasionally, someone has pushed the wrong button, and I just needed to vent to someone about it. Then that some*one* turned into some *people*. Vent is just a kinder word that allows you to feel justified in telling a story that probably made another person look really bad and portrayed you as an angel. Ladies, admit it: when we get mad, we get vicious. Dictionary.com defines venting as, "The small hole at the breach of a gun through which the charge is ignited." It only takes something small to ignite something deadly.

James 3:5–6 gives a great analogy of how much damage one word can do:

> It only takes a spark, remember, to set off a forest fire. A careless or wrongly placed word out of your mouth can do that. By our speech we can ruin the world, turn harmony to chaos, throw mud on a reputation, send the whole world up in smoke and go up in smoke with it, smoke right from the pit of hell. (MSG)

We've all heard the phrase, "what goes around, comes around. Yeah, it comes all the way back around to you. Remember that people watch what you do and say. What does bad-mouthing someone else do for your reputation? Girls tend to trash other girls behind their back and while pretending to be friends to their face. Guys don't do that.

They will tell you to your face. But since we see girls acting this way, we know: beware." Do I have your attention yet?

The truth is, we've all been hurt by someone else's words, and we've all turned around and said something that ended up hurting someone else. The cycle has to end somewhere.

How do you stop? Well, it takes discipline. I try to find the good in someone or in something she has done. Let me give you an example. Say someone had a solo in church, and a friend said to me, "Man, she did not sound good!" Whether it was the truth or not, in order to kill the gossip and not put that person down, I'd say something like, "Well, hey, at least they can get up there and sing. I don't even have the guts to do that, so more props to them!" When it comes to loving your enemies—one of the hardest things for me to do—sometimes I literally look in the mirror and repeat good things about that person and say that I love him or her. Before I know it (and this is based off of experience), I really do care about that person without faking it, and I see the good in her without forcing it. If someone hurts me or makes me mad, and I'm tempted to vent to my roommate or best friend, I bring up a different subject, even though it's hard, just to get my mind off of it and forget what I was going to say. Then when I'm alone I pray about it, even screaming into my pillow and writing in my journal just to blow out the fuse! It takes discipline, but I assure you that it becomes easier the more you do it.

I have a few mentors in my life—my mom being one of them—who I'll confide in and then take my issue straight to the person I'm upset with. When confronting the person you felt offended by, make sure you say "I" and not "you." For example, "I feel hurt by the way this came across. You might not have meant to say it like that, but that's how I feel." Do not say, "you yelled at me, and you were wrong, and you did this, this, and this!" Trust me you will get better results with the first example. If you want to see change, that change has to start with you sowing words of life into someone else. Remember, "What goes around, comes back around." I want to see you quenching the fire, not fanning the flame.

> A bit in the mouth of a horse controls the whole horse. A small rudder on a huge ship in the hands of a skilled captain sets a course in the face of the strongest winds. A word out of

> your mouth may seem of no account, but it can accomplish nearly anything—or destroy it!
> (James 3:3–4, MSG)

What say you?

- What is gossip to you?
- Do you have a tendency towards gossip?
- Do you choose your words carefully? Are you paying attention to what you say and to whom you are saying it?

EPISODE 34
No Dead Ends *by Suzette Perlmutter*

Have you ever examined your life and asked, "Is this it? Is this all there is to life?" I asked myself this question recently, and I felt God speak to me with a very profound and marvelous answer, "No, this is not it." I think of how easy it is to settle into a mundane lifestyle that seems to repeat itself day in and day out. We get up, go to work or school, come home and fix dinner, and then go to bed to get up in the morning and do it all over again.

I remember going through the routine when I graduated from college. I became a schoolteacher, and for my first two years of teaching, all I did was come home to an empty apartment every day. I was so unhappy, even becoming depressed. Was this all my life would be? Is this all God was going to do with my life? There had to be more. Please, Lord God in Heaven, let there be more. I realized I didn't want my life to be meaningless, so I prayed a lot and searched my soul. I found that the key was to look outside my own loneliness and see that so many people are in the same dullness as I was. They also need someone to show them that this is not all there is to life.

There are no dead ends with God, only mile markers. You get to one stage of life, and then move to the next, always learning something from each. I learned that this meant taking risks to meet new people and get involved in life again.

Personally, I feel like God led me to become really involved as a single woman: going to young adults services, becoming apart of Velo's women's ministry, and becoming a home group leader for college students. I allowed myself to become vulnerable in meeting new people and eventually getting into a position of leadership where I had to lean on the Lord for every word I spoke and every move I made, so I could make sure it was all in his name and for his glory. I was so busy doing the Lord's work that I hardly had the time to feel sorry for myself. Instead, I learned how much I loved to love people. What a joy it brought to my life.

A few years later I got married, and God slowed my schedule of duties down to focus on the construction and foundation laying of the first year of my marriage. As I write this, I am still in my first year of marriage. I have been blessed with an amazing husband and a blissful first year. However, I found myself asking again, "Is this it?" I have waited and waited all my life to get married, now is this it? Was my ministering over? Was my time to work for God done? Again, the answer was no.

The answer to the question of "Is this it?" is always no. God has actually incorporated my husband into supporting me while I continue to work with Velo. God has shown my husband and me a ministering future together. God has a plan for each of us. His will is that no one perishes, so our work won't be done until he comes back to take us home.

My encouragement to you today is for you to know that whatever your stage of life—whether single or married, a pastor or just a church attendee—God is not done with you. He is faithful to the completion of the work he has begun in you. There is more for you to do before you go to Heaven, so start trying new things and never discount your contribution. No matter how big or small your gift to the Lord, he sees it all. View everyone as needing Jesus as much as you do. Such fulfillment will grow in your heart. Peacefulness will come. Though you know you aren't perfect, you are doing your part to fulfill the plan that God has for you.

> … being confident of this, that he who began a good work in you will carry it on to completion until the day of Christ Jesus.
> (Philippians 1:6, NIV)

What say you?

- Are you faithful to the Lord's work? Is your life fruitful?
- Are you waiting for anything that could be holding you back?
- How can you begin to make positive contributions to people and organizations that are valuable to you?

EPISODE 35
The Road Less Traveled *by Kristie K. McCrary*

In a small flat in London on April 13, 1742, George Frederic Handel completed the most famous oratorio ever composed. To this day, the anointed work of art is consistently performed in concert halls all over the world.

In 1741, after enjoying decades of success, Handel's popularity plummeted because the Church of England opposed his performances, which were based on biblical themes, in secular theaters. If that wasn't enough, rival opera companies took a large number of his once loyal ticket holders. By the age of fifty-six, Handel had become overwhelmed by debt and faced an almost guaranteed stint in the dreaded debtor's prison. His failing health and inability to draw a consistent and enthusiastic audience forced him to give his final performance in London.

Growing up with a stern and practical father—a surgeon and barber by trade—was difficult for the gifted Handle. His father was fixed on sending his son to law school. Although Handel was extraordinarily talented, he forbade him from taking any type of music lessons until Handel caught an unexpected break. Around the age of nine, a duke heard Handel play the organ after a worship service and convinced Handel's father to provide him with extensive musical training. Handel's career immediately catapulted, but his father was never completely satisfied or supportive.

I have to believe that, on the day of Handel's last performance in London, faced with the realization that his career was over prematurely, he likely reflected back to when he was a small child and his father's advice had been to take the more practical road and career. Instead, Handel had pursued the desire of his heart and chosen the road less traveled. There was a spark of hope in the midst of Handel's storm. He had just inherited a commission from Dublin charity to compose a special project for an upcoming benefit. During the same time frame, his friend, Charles Jensen, presented him with a libretto to complete that had been written about the life of Christ. Handel decided to merge the two projects together.

On August 22, Handel embarked on what would become the most anointed and powerful oratorio. His house servant faithfully prepared trays of food and, for three weeks, carried three meals a day back and forth from his master's rooms, yet the meals were barely touched. Handel camped out in his room like a hermit. Near the close of the twenty-fourth day, all two hundred sixty pages of *The Messiah* were complete. The Dublin benefit where it premiered on April 13, 1742, raised four hundred pounds and freed 142 men from debtor's prison. The oratorio continued to raise funds for charity throughout the remainder of Handel's life.

What if Handel had not gathered enough courage to follow his heart and take the road less traveled? Billions of people would not have had the privilege of enjoying the most fantastic oratorio ever composed, *The Messiah*.

Handel had to make a difficult decision in order to achieve his destiny. He had to take a stand and say, "Dad, you're my family, and I love you very much, but I know what I have been born to do. I know what my destiny is, and I have to pursue it." As with Handel, a time will come when we also have to grow up and personally listen to the voice of the Lord. That's when we begin to see our destiny more clearly.

> Jesus said, "If? There are no 'ifs' among believers. Anything can happen.'"
> (Mark 9:23, MSG)

What say you?

- Being a composer and musician made Handel's heart race. What makes your heart race?
- Do you know your destiny or have an idea of what it is? Are you willing to pursue it?
- Are you listening to the Lord personally, or are you leaning on others to hear the voice of the Lord for you?

EPISODE 36
The Blessing Secret *by Julie Couch*

We hear about blessings all the time. People pray for blessings and expect them to come. This is scriptural. However, the blessing secret is that you must live a holy and righteous life to obtain the blessings. You must live a life of obedience.

Everything in the world is already God's. This means that everything in the world is already available to us, if we are only obedient. If you are obedient to God's word and to his will, all you have to do is command something to happen, and it will. But do not think that you can live any way you desire, doing anything your flesh wants, and still expect God's blessings.

According to Deuteronomy 28:1–2:

> If you listen obediently to the Voice of God, your God, and heartily obey all his commandments that I command you today, God, your God, will place you on high, high above all the nations of the world. All these blessings will come down on you and spread out beyond you because you have responded to the Voice of God, your God. (MSG)

The chapter goes on to say that believers will be blessed in the city, in the country, and everywhere they go. It also points out that the disobedient will bring curses upon their lives. But, many times, the key to this passage is overlooked. Yes, you have to be obedient to be blessed, but in order to be obedient, you must first hear God's voice. We must learn to listen to the voice of God. Then we must learn to be obedient to his words so we may inherit his blessings.

Deuteronomy 30:1–7 states that if we become disobedient, it is not too late to turn back. It says:

> While you are out among the nations where God has dispersed you and the blessings and curses come in just the way I have set them before you, and you and your children take them seriously and come back to God, your God, and obey him with your whole heart and soul according to everything that I command you today, God, your God, will restore everything you

> lost; he'll have compassion on you; he'll come back and pick up the pieces from all the places where you were scattered. No matter how far away you end up, God, your God, will get you out of there and bring you back to the land your ancestors once possessed. It will be yours again. He will give you a good life and make you more numerous than your ancestors.
>
> God, your God, will cut away the thick calluses on your heart and your children's hearts, freeing you to love God, your God, with your whole heart and soul and live, really live. God, your God, will put all these curses on your enemies who hated you and were out to get you.
>
> And you will make a new start, listening obediently to God, keeping all his commandments that I am commanding you today. (MSG)

Obedience is not only required when it is convenient. Our lives should model obedience. You see, obedience will stretch us and bring us to new levels in our walk with Christ. Think about Noah, Moses, Esther, and so many other Bible heroes. Their entire lives were altered and blessed due to their willingness to obey. This is the blessing secret that will bring rewards beyond expectation. If we listen intently to God's voice for direction and we live a holy, righteous life of obedience, we will be blessed beyond measure. The blessings are already ours. God is just waiting for us to be fully obedient.

> If any of you wants to serve me, then follow me. Then you'll be where I am, ready to serve at a moment's notice. The Father will honor and reward anyone who serves me.
> (John 12:26, MSG)

What say you?

- Have you ever made the decision not to obey God?
- Did you experience consequences from your disobedience?
- Is it easy or difficult for you to obey God?

EPISODE 37
Listen … You'll Hear It *by Courtney Bodine*

When you stop and think about the power of God, it is so amazing. There is nowhere that you can go where he is not.

God is continuously tugging at the strings of our hearts to get our attention. When we listen to his voice, we will undoubtedly uncover a truth that we have never understood or we will be encouraged by his grace. The moments when we listen we restore our spirits and heal our souls. How often do you really take the time to be still and rest in his presence?

When I got married, I started attending a church of a different denomination than that of the church I grew up in. Naturally, I wanted to continue going to church in the atmosphere that I was comfortable with, but after a lot of prayer, I dove into the unfamiliar setting. It was definitely a different atmosphere than I was used to, but I did my best to keep an open mind. After a few weeks of visiting, I started to feel out of place. I didn't know anyone, and the worship and style of the services were both very different than anything I had experienced. I would not say that I ever had a bad attitude toward this denomination, but I was indifferent to it.

After we had been attending for about a month, the preacher delivered a message about the power of prayer. He broke The Lord's Prayer down line by line. When he got to the point in the prayer about debts ("Forgive us our debts as we forgive our debtors"), he discussed how we could become so thoughtless as we say these words. I began thinking, *Please forgive me for what I have done, and I'm going to forgive those who have wronged me*—that's what we're supposed to be thinking when we pray those words.

When I wrapped my mind around this, I knew that God was trying to tell me something. I realized that I had been harboring bitterness in my heart toward a person whom I had a difficult time getting along with. I've always been aware of my bitterness toward that person, but I never felt the need to let go of it. I honestly didn't want to let go of it—I didn't feel ready. But in my sensitivity to the Holy Spirit in that moment, God spoke to me, and I realized that it was high time to begin the process of forgiving and healing.

As I thanked God for revealing this to me and continued to be responsive and open to his voice, he brought another point to my attention. He said to me, "I can speak to you anywhere. Listen." In that moment, I realized how wrong I had been in my attitude toward a setting that I was not used to. Who was I to underestimate the power of God? Of course God can speak to me and touch me no matter where I am. I simply hadn't been listening.

In fact, God revealed things of such great importance to me in a place where I felt slightly isolated and distant. Although we sometimes feel this way, God is never far away. If you just trust God, and continually listen to his voice, He may surprise you. We should strive to live our lives in a constant state of praise and prayer to God. Always listen. He is constantly trying to speak to us.

> For God speaks again and again, though people do not recognize it.
> (Job 33:14, NLT)

What say you?

- Is there someone you haven't forgiven?
- Are you listening to God at all times, in all surroundings, and in every situation?
- How do you hear the voice of God?

EPISODE 38
The Blessing *by Naomi Noy*

I love to pray for blessings over people in my life but never thought much about praying for a blessing on myself until I recently stumbled across a verse in 1 Samuel 30:6, which reads, "And David was greatly distressed... but David encouraged himself in the Lord his God" (KJV).

That's when it dawned on me—David not only encouraged himself in the Lord by praying for blessings on his life, but Jabez did as well. Since my discovery, I have made the prayer blessing part of my regular time with the Lord, and it has made a significant difference in my life.

I want to share a prayer blessing I recently wrote, and I pray that it will bless and encourage you.

> Dear God,
>
> I know many people will read these words. However, no one bigger than you, more important than you, greater than you, or even equal to you, will ever read this as you do.
>
> God, your love is so amazing! I am so grateful that you have sent the Holy Spirit as my comforter and Jesus Christ as my deliver. Please Lord, anoint me and bless me with an overflowing measure of love, joy, and peace so that I will be a vessel, example, and light to direct and lead others to you, Jesus. Lord help me to have the heart of Jabez, who said, "'Oh, that thou wouldest bless me indeed, and enlarge my coast, and that thine hand might be with me, and that thou wouldest keep me from evil, that it may not grieve me!' And God granted him that which he requested." 1 Chronicles 4:10 (KJV).
>
> Thank you, God, for forgiving me of my sin and delivering me from Satan.
>
> I am also thankful, God, for the women at Velo. In moments where I have felt so alone, unworthy, and unloved, these women have been there to give me a

tangible hug, to say an audible prayer, and to share a visible smile and tear. Lord, I know what your word says for me to do: to have faith, believe, hope, and expect to marry the man you have chosen for me. However, in the meantime, I know that the birthing pains I am pushing and stretching through are not in vain.

I celebrate John 16:21–22:

> A woman, when she gives birth to a child, has grief (anguish, agony) because her time has come. But when she has delivered the child, she no longer remembers her pain (trouble, anguish) because she is so glad that a man (a child, a human being) has been born into the world. So for the present you are also in sorrow (in distress and depressed); but I will see you again and [then] your hearts will rejoice, and no one can take from you your joy (gladness, delight). (AB)

I know that my situation has not come to stay, but shall pass. It is here to birth something—a miracle. I thank you, Lord, God, Jesus, Father, Son, and Holy Spirit in one, that the birth pains are here with urgency. Thank you, God, for being on time and for blessing me indeed.

Dear Heavenly Father, bless those who read this prayer in Jesus name.

Amen.

P.S. I love you!

The first thing I want you to do is pray. Pray every way you know how, for everyone you know.
(1 Timothy 2:1, MSG)

What say you?

- Who are you blessing today?
- Do you ask the Lord for personal favors and blessings?
- How do you pray?

EPISODE 39

Road Rules *by Kristie K. McCrary*

There's a new and reevaluated meaning to the phrase "Wolves in sheep's clothing."

Jesus preached his Sermon on the Mount to a large crowd, including the disciples. His sermon focused on living a life of discipline and awareness of your enemies. Many Bible scholars consider this sermon to be the road rules to living a Christian life. From The Lord's prayer to requirements like "Do unto others," "turn the other cheek," "cast not your pearls before swine," and "the salt of the earth," the Sermon on the Mount, recorded in Matthew 5–7, is extraordinarily valuable to living and understanding the Christian walk.

Jesus continues his teaching, addressing false prophets, "Watch out for false prophets. They come to you in sheep's clothing, but inwardly they are ferocious wolves" (Matthew 7:15, NIV). This heads-up metaphor is key to understanding the world we live in today.

I consider the words "false prophet" to encompass much more than the term "prophet" usually means. In the theater of my mind, the term represents fence-sitting Christians—the ones who play the game and don't always strive to do what the word of God tells them to do. I know we're all human, and we are tempted and make mistakes from time to time. However, the Christian's I'm talking about have mastered living in the grey, as if they're living two different lives. Those are the people that we have to be so careful about. They can get to us and drag us down. That's why Jesus refers to them, in the Sermon on the Mount, as wolves. To paraphrase, he was saying, "Hey, wake up, gang. There's wolves in sheep's clothing, hanging with you and sitting inside your comfort zone."

Wolves are members of the predator family. They survive mostly by killing and eating other animals, making their home wherever their prey lives. The two main causes of death for wolves are fighting with wolves within their pack, and fighting with other wolf packs over territory. These facts alone cast wolves in a negative light. Are you familiar with the popular phrase, "I felt like I was in the middle of a pack of wolves?" Wherever wolves are mentioned, there's trouble.

As children, we learned about the sly and self-centered ways of wolves through timeless stories, such as "Little Red Riding Hood." The little girl was warned by her mother not to mess around in the forest because of danger. However, she ignored her mother's words and ran into a wolf, which disguised his voice as friendly. Later, the girl arrived at her grandmother's to discover that the wolf that she had encountered earlier had eaten her grandmother ... not to mention that the wolf came after her next!

I realize this is a children's story, but it offers a great lesson. Beware of the wolves in your life and pay attention to warnings. So many of us go through this scenario in our real lives. We're warned over and over again, and we continue to ignore the signs. The wolves in our lives have the ability to disguise their voices, appearances, and anything else they can think of to try and distract us and trip us up.

They're master chameleons and become whatever they need to fit the situation they face. We need to be very careful with whom and where we spend our time. What we put inside ourselves will always come out. What are you putting into yourself? What do you watch? What do you listen to? Where and with whom are you spending time? Your dreams, your purpose, and your destiny will all come from what you put in. "Become wise by walking with the wise; hang out with fools and watch your life fall to pieces" (Proverbs 13:20, MSG).

Beware of the grey areas and the people in our circles who are fence sitters. We need to love and pray for them, but we must realize that they can be like wolves in sheep's clothing with the ability to distract us and lead us in the wrong direction.

Pay attention to the road rules in Matthew 5–7, and I guarantee you that you will have a safe and pleasant journey.

> So if you're serious about living this new resurrection life with Christ, act like it. Pursue the things over which Christ presides. Don't shuffle along, eyes to the ground, absorbed with the things right in front of you. Look up, and be alert to what is going on around Christ---that's where the action is. See things from his perspective.
> (Colossians 3:1-2, MSG)

What say you?

- What are you putting into yourself? What do you watch? What do you listen to?
- With whom do you spend the majority of your time and where? Are there any wolves in your life?
- How can you improve on your road rules?

EPISODE 40

Next Time *by Khia Paige*

"You have the right to remain silent. If you give up that right, anything you say can and will be used against you in a court of law."

"Well, congratulations, Miss Paige. You are now a juvenile delinquent. The pioneers who went before you will be so proud. You are a role model to the faithful followers who will come after you. You are now a statistic—part of a vicious cycle that perpetuates, again and again." I was bombarded with statistics about the percentage of youth who commit crimes and become repeat offenders, developing a lifetime of antisocial disordered behavior. The juvenile detention center social worker gave me a scared-straight pep talk when I was released.

"Okay, Paige, we will keep your deluxe cell and bunk bed reserved for your next visit. See you next time." The social worker said, smiling mockingly and waving goodbye to me. *Next time?* The devil is a liar. There would never be a next time.

The most humbling period in my life occurred immediately after making a series of terrible choices, getting caught red-handed in a string of misdeeds. I let Satan make a big fool out of me. I began to believe that I had lost my calling to be a missionary. I just knew that God could never use me. I didn't have the nerve to look my brokenhearted parents in the eye.

Maybe you have also made some inappropriate decisions, leading to consequences that are not God's plan for you. It is easy to trust God and believe in his grace when we are blameless and innocent. What about when we are guilty? I was guilty far beyond reasonable doubt. Let me explain.

The wealthiest I have ever been was when I was a sophomore in high school. Over the course of two and a half months, I made almost $63,000 by marketing and distributing black-market items. Life became complicated. I was too tense to sleep at night. I was constantly looking over my shoulder, and my customers were so demanding it just about wore me out. This was the most overwhelming period in my childhood. I was sixteen years old, but I felt thirty. One day, things turned ugly, and I found myself behind bars.

In court, I stood, prepared for the worst, before a stern judge. All charges were dropped, and I was put on probation. This was a miracle I definitely didn't deserve. The Lord spoke to me and instructed me to give all the remaining cash to missions. In my spirit, I knew that I was symbolically sowing my own future as a missionary. I gave all of my nice clothes, jewelry, and luxury items to Goodwill. For the fist time in my life, I got a real job. Of course, the only work I was qualified for as a teenager was unskilled labor. I became an honorable member of the McDonald's team. I worked hard for pennies, literally. Strangely, I felt like a kid again—God had restored my childhood. I was saved and had received a special prayer language. I believed God's word, but I was still not delivered. My deliverance was not birthed until I renounced every negative thing spoken over me that was not of God.

I encourage all of you to do the same. Accept and believe what God says about your future. If someone says something about your life, it needs to be parallel with the word of God. If not, then the person's words should go back into the pits of hell from whence they came.

Our sins and mistakes are never beyond God's forgiveness and grace. Upon receiving deliverance, God lifted my head. I had dignity once again. Do not be ashamed of your past. It is because of our pasts that we have the testimony that God will use to set others free.

> But You, O Lord, are a shield for me, my glory, and the lifter of my head.
> (Psalm 3:3, AB)

What say you?

- Have you found it difficult to forgive yourself? Does the shame of your past define and limit you?
- Do you feel that past sins have jeopardized your future and your dreams?
- Do you believe and understand the power of God's forgiveness and grace? Do you believe in complete restoration?

EPISODE 41

I Am Righteous *by Aunie Brooks*

After studying student achievement results from the previous year, a low-achieving school district researched strategies to improve their program. They soon devised an experiment, which proved very successful in the end. Like any valid experiment, the school's involved only one variable: human expectations.

The district randomly selected five teachers and one hundred students. These teachers and students were told by the district officials that they were the brightest in their respecting fields. Each teacher was assigned a class of twenty students in an attempt to create the best classes and produce the best results in the district. What was the result of the experiment? At the end of the year, the selected students' test scores were an entire 30 percent higher than the scores of their peers. These teachers taught in the same buildings they had taught in before, with the same resources they had had in the past, teaching the same students they had known for years. The only things that changed were the expectations of both the teachers and the students.

People rise to the level that they perceive they are able to reach. This can be good, or it can be bad. Expectation can be the oxygen that allows one spark of fire to leap into a roaring flame, or it can be the snuffer that stifles the energy of that same spark. Everything depends on perception. Unfortunately, this truth acts as a snuffer for many Christians. We simply can't perceive ourselves as anything greater than sinners.

True, we believe that we are sinners saved by grace, but we are still sinners. Yes, we have a heart willing and ready to please God. But we half expect to fail because we believe ourselves to be hopeless sinners. So, through a self-prescribing life of sin, we go on sinning. Why? It's because we perceive ourselves to be sinners.

What if we change our perceptions of ourselves to mirror the perception God has of us? 2 Corinthians 5:21 declares, "God made him who had no sin to be sin for us, so that in him we might become the righteousness of God" (NIV). You and I are the righteousness of God. And as Webster's Dictionary would argue, a righteous sinner is an oxymoron. After all, righteous means "without sin." Psalm 1:5 and

Romans 5:19 echo the truth that one cannot be called "righteous" and also be called a "sinner." With this in mind, meditate on the knowledge that through Christ's sacrifice we are declared righteous. We are no longer sinners. Through Christ's power we can live righteous lives.

Read those last few lines as many times as you need to. Read it until it sinks into the core of who you are, until it changes your perception of who you are.

It is important to note that the scripture does not assert that, by perceiving yourself to be righteous, you can attain perfection, never sinning again. It does mean, however, that you are separate from sin, unattached to it, which allows you to possess boldness and confidence to refuse sin in any given situation. What a humbling, and yet empowering, truth.

Imagine how this world would change if every Christian perceived himself or herself as righteous. Imagine just how righteous our world would truly be. The truth is, people rise to the level that they perceive they are able to reach. Perceive yourselves as righteous, sinless women, and live accordingly.

> God made him who had no sin to be sin for us, so that in him we might become the righteousness of God.
> (2 Corinthians 5:21, NIV)

What say you?

- How do you perceive yourself?
- Do you believe that you can and do live as a righteous person?

EPISODE 42
What's a Girl to Do? *by Jennifer L. Oldham*

Do you ever wonder how Jesus did it? How he was able to walk this earth sinless and completely focused on his mission? The fact that Jesus lived his whole life and never sinned—not even once—is mind-boggling to me. That part of the story is easier to skim over, because if you try to wrap your mind around Jesus' sinless ness, it simply doesn't seem possible.

I can't make it a week, a day, and let's face it, some days not even to lunch without feeling temptation. Honestly, I just want to give in sometimes. I can tell you story after story of how God has been faithful to me, yet here I am—twenty-four years and a Bible college degree later, and at times, I actually entertain the idea of throwing it all away because … it's hard. So if Jesus was human—just like you and me—and was tempted in every way—just as we are tempted—and yet was without sin, I want to know his secret. How did he do it?

The Bible says that it was the joy set before Jesus that caused him to endure the cross. Joy? The Message translation says:

> Keep your eyes on Jesus, who both began and finished this race we're in. Study how he did it. Because he never lost sight of where he was headed—that exhilarating finish in and with God—he could put up with anything along the way: cross, shame, whatever. And now he's there, in the place of honor, right alongside God. When you find yourselves flagging in your faith, go over that story again, item by item, that long litany of hostility he plowed through. That will shoot adrenaline into your souls! (Hebrews 12:2–3, MSG)

Jesus never lost sight of the goal, and we can't lose sight of Jesus.

> For now we are looking in a mirror that gives only a dim (blurred) reflection [of reality as in a riddle or enigma], but then [when perfection comes] we shall see in reality and face to face! Now I know in part (imperfectly), but then I shall know and understand fully and clearly, even in the same manner as I have

> been fully and clearly known and understood [by God]. (1 Corinthians 13:12, AB)

You see, Jesus was able to see beyond the here and now to the big picture. He knew that our present sufferings are not even worth comparing to the glory that is to be revealed.

If you're like me, you probably find yourself running on caffeine more often than on faith. You may be wondering how you're going to make it out of your latest mess. If you've ever woken up and dreaded going to work because your dream job turned out to be just another dead end, you've found out Mr. Right couldn't have been more wrong, or you're still wondering when exactly happily-ever-after begins, there's a good chance that the women around you have taken that train a time or two as well.

What's a girl to do? Well, for starters, you get out of bed and go to work. Stop looking for Mr. Right, and learn how to love by practicing at every chance you get. You realize that ever after is really right now.

> So we're not giving up. How could we! Even though on the outside it often looks like things are falling apart on us, on the inside, where God is making new life, not a day goes by without his unfolding grace. These hard times are small potatoes compared to the coming good times, the lavish celebration prepared for us. There's far more here than meets the eye. The things we see now are here today, gone tomorrow. But the things we can't see now will last forever.
> (2 Corinthians 4:16–18, MSG)

What say you?

- Are you trying to make people, jobs, and things into your sources of fulfillment, or are you opting for God as your source?
- Do you have faith to see beyond the present and trust that God sees the big picture? Or are you camping out in your valley, unwilling to change?

EPISODE 43
The Champ Meets the Chump *by Kristie K. McCrary*

If we're going to become champions—or champs—we've got to focus on the big picture and the reality of our dreams. Becoming champs also requires some sacrifice and willingness to stay in the right relationships. We can't afford to spend quality time with the chumps even as comfortable as they are to be around. They are people-pleasers, constantly trying to get a good laugh or possibly playing the blame game, listen to what someone else says to them rather than what God is trying to say to them. Sadly, chumps are set up for failure because of an incorrect mentality and thought process. Let's look at an example of a chump in Mark 10 and how a wrong mentality changed the course of his life.

> As he went out into the street, a man came running up, greeted him with great reverence, and asked, "Good Teacher, what must I do to get eternal life?"
> Jesus said, "Why are you calling me good? No one is good, only God. You know the commandments: Don't murder, don't commit adultery, don't steal, don't lie, don't cheat, honor your father and mother."
> He said, "Teacher, I have—from my youth—kept them all!"
> Jesus looked him hard in the eye—and loved him! He said, "There's one thing left: Go sell whatever you own and give it to the poor. All your wealth will then be heavenly wealth. And come follow me."
> The man's face clouded over. This was the last thing he expected to hear, and he walked off with a heavy heart. He was holding on tight to a lot of things, and not about to let go.
> Looking at his disciples, Jesus said, "Do you have any idea how difficult it is for people who 'have it all' to enter God's kingdom?" The disciples couldn't believe what they were hearing, but Jesus kept on: "You can't imagine how difficult. I'd say it's easier for a camel to

> go through a needle's eye than for the rich to get into God's kingdom."
> That set the disciples back on their heels. "Then who has any chance at all?" they asked.
> Jesus was blunt: "No chance at all if you think you can pull it off by yourself. Every chance in the world if you let God do it." Mark 10:17–27 (MSG)

This poor guy just didn't get it. A chump, exactly like the rich young man in Mark, is unaware of the destiny that lies ahead. He lacks the wisdom and insight needed to do the right thing at the right time for the right purpose. He's usually busy acting silly and continuing to miss out on the race of life, completely unaware of the price and dedication required to succeed. Sadly, the chump never experiences the thrill of victory, because he gets frustrated when times get tough and lacks the endurance needed to keep running and stay focused on the race that will eventually lead him to his destiny.

On the other hand, there's the champ. A champ is a person with solid convictions and focus who knows that the life he lives will eventually lead him to his destiny. He concentrates on holiness and has learned that holiness is not the way to get to God but is what happens in his heart after he's really gotten to know the Lord. Champs aren't perfect. They make mistakes and experience regrets just like the chumps. What separates the two is that the champ understands restoration and has the ability to move forward rather than simply look back at the past.

Champs understand that Jesus died so that the consequences of our sins would not separate us from our destiny. Champs are continually thankful for the blessings and forgiveness of God in their lives. I believe that's the real key to their success and tenacity. They're thankful for grace that they receive in weak moments and for anointing that they receive in ministry moments, jobs, health, and unlimited opportunities. Even when they feel weary and worn out, they never give up or stop running. That's the mentality of a champ.

Let's try to follow in the footsteps of a champ. In weak moments, find the conviction inside to keep running towards destiny. When we come to the understanding that we can't become champs in our own strength and that God is the only one who can accelerate our lives and the roads to our destinies, we put ourselves in the best position we can find. Let's stay patient and steadfast and allow God to work things out for us. By God's grace, we are champs.

> But principled people hold tight, keep a firm grip on life, sure that their clean, pure hands will get stronger and stronger! (Job 17:9, MSG)

What say you?

- Do you have some tendencies of a chump? Are you insecure, unsettled, or a people-pleaser?
- Do you have the mentality of the champ? Do you concentrate on the race and running towards your destiny? Are you positioning yourself for greatness?
- How do you balance relevance with holiness in your life?

EPISODE 44
Choose to Choose *by Cindy R. Wood*

Obtaining victory in Jesus requires a lot, from prayer to divine appointments. One such appointment was with my mentor, who challenged me with a question I will never forget: "What is the one thing you do all of your waking life?"

Puzzled, I just sat there for a moment. "Breathe?"

"No," she replied, "You can hold your breath." Oh. Hey, I got it, I thought.

"I go to the restroom."

"Not so much," she told me. "Babies, kids, and even some adults, wear diapers." So that wasn't it.

She slowly asked me the question again. "What is the one thing that you do all of your waking life?" I racked my brain for things I do all of the time. Still nothing came to mind.

"You're doing it now," she said patiently. "Think about it, Cindy. Are you looking to the left or right? Are you tapping your foot? Are you adjusting the phone next to your ear?"

I laughed and said, "Yeah, actually, I'm doing all those things."

Then it clicked.

"I am choosing to do all of those things."

She exclaimed laughter like a proud teacher. "Right. The one thing you do all of your waking life is choose." So I chose to stay on the phone and talk with her, and chose to scratch my head and roll my eyes. I felt a bit silly for not answering in one guess, but it was worth it. What a revelation.

Everything we do requires a choice. From eating to sleeping to your job or your education to hanging out with the wrong crowd or staying at home to not choosing to do anything—each reflects a choice.

The Bible is full of references to when God's people made good choices; I think Joshua said it best:

> And if it seems evil to you to serve the Lord, choose for yourselves this day whom you will serve, whether the gods which your fathers served that *were* on the other side of the River, or the gods of the Amorites, in

> whose land you dwell. But as for me and my house,
> we will serve the Lord. (Joshua 24:15, NKJV)

Praise God! Joshua knew what made a truly great leader—good choices! Regardless of his circumstances, Joshua chose to serve the Lord. If we want to obtain victory, we have to choose to trust in the Lord and serve him completely. You know, Jesus actually gives us this choice as well.

John 10:10 states, "The thief cometh not, but for to steal, and to kill, and to destroy: I am come that they might have life, and that they might have it more abundantly" (KJV). Hello, anybody home?

Every day, I choose to have a good day. Does that actually happen every day? Um … no. Sure, bad things may make me sad, angry, upset, or even disappointed. Through it all, I choose to trust in the Lord. I choose to speak God's word over my life and rejoice, knowing that God is in control. I am sure everyone has made bad choices once or twice in life. I know I have.

Throughout my life, I have learned that the best choice anyone can make to cover a lifetime of bad choices is the choice to serve Jesus. Without Jesus, we would all be nothing. Without his guidance, we are lost. Without his help, we are destined for failure.

Besides, knowing the amazing love God has for us, why would we choose anything else?

> And hope does not disappoint us, because God has poured out his love into our hearts by the Holy Spirit, whom he has given us.
> (Romans 5:5, NIV)

What say you?

- What kind of choices are you making today? Are they life-changing and relevant?
- How does your attitude affect your choices?
- Are you choosing God?

EPISODE 45
Breakthrough *by Missy Lares*

I think we can all agree that our finances can bring stress and anxiety. Some people are better with money than others. I can say this is not one of my strong points. You may have come to a realization that you want to change, but how do you change what you have been doing throughout your whole life? Now all of a sudden God has exposed to you an area in your life that you have always been in control of, and now it has to be surrendered.

Finance was never a concern of mine. I thought everything was going well in my life. One day he opened my eyes and ears and started speaking to my spirit about money and breakthrough. During this period I was longing for areas of my life to change and be renewed, but I didn't know how to make it happen.

He spoke so clearly to me, saying, "I can't break through until you give me everything." I had thought that I had whole-heartedly given him every area of my life. During this period, my pastor also spoke on Wednesday nights on this very same subject. I thought it was a coincidence, but the Lord reassured me that it wasn't.

You see, I grew up in a Christian home, learning to pay a 10 percent tithe at a very early age, but that wasn't the problem. I lived beyond my means, not giving my offerings. But the paycheck we get weekly, biweekly or evenly monthly is not ours, it's His. The Lord gives to us so we can give to others. The problem is that if we're in debt we can't be a blessing. Malachi 3:10 challenges us by saying, "'Bring the whole tithe into the storehouse, that there may be food in my house. Test me in this,' says the Lord Almighty, 'and see if I will not throw open the floodgates of heaven and pour out so much blessing that you will not have room enough for it'" (NIV).

God wants us to live in freedom and in his promises. I believe our selfishness often stands in the way. To get to our hearts, God has to gain access to our treasures. Once our treasures are his, then he can break through. God is the father of the breakthrough. His word does not return void. Will you challenge him today?

> For where your treasure is, there your heart will be also. (Matthew 6:21, NIV)

What say you?

- What area of your finances do you need to surrender?
- Do you tithe regularly to your local church, other ministries, and to missions?
- When you receive your paycheck, what first crosses your mind—your bills or your tithe?

EPISODE 46
Living Beyond Yourself *by Amy Blevins*

One of the tenets of Velo is to be authentic. If we aspire to fulfill our mission of becoming authentic women of God, then it is imperative that we be honest with ourselves and with God about why we spend God's money the way that we do.

As Christian women, we risk unfulfilled spiritual and emotional talents. It all hinges on our attitudes towards money and the uncertainty of living beyond ourselves. The good news is that it's not too late to redeem what we've lost and turn from despair to hope. We can step from fallow ground onto fertile ground. I'm learning that we honor God as much by what we don't do, as by what we do. So how can we honor God by what we don't do with our finances? Proverbs is full of scriptures that sound like "the wise man does, while the foolish man does…."

I believe we can honor God by examining where we spend our money. If we spend compulsively, we should ask for discernment to recognize when and why and then allow God to resolve our anxieties. If we spend frivolously, we should confess that to God and allow the Holy Spirit to help us develop self-control and contentment. If we've camped out in denial, it's time to be honest—we are afraid, overwhelmed, and don't know where to start. We must allow God to help us overcome our fears. God will provide for our needs in the right order, and the right time, transforming us, by the grace of God, from foolish women to wise women.

Is it scary to be honest, to be that vulnerable and transparent with God? Frankly, it's scarier to be honest with ourselves. You see, God already knows. He is just waiting for us to accept ownership of our part in the circumstance and ask for his help. He has made provision for each one of us, and his word says that we experience new mercies every day. The Holy Spirit compels us to surrender things to God so that we can experience freedom.

This is not a message of judgment but of freedom. If we know that our attitudes toward money do not honor God, change starts when we confess to the Lord and ask for his help. Since we have free will, we must put feet to our faith. We must take the first step toward his will, and God will meet us. So, be encouraged, our god-given dreams and visions for our lives are within reach if we're willing to submit our lives to the Lord and allow him to direct our steps.

God wants to prove himself to you in every way.

Without God, the Bible is just a book; its words have no power if they can't be applied and bear fruit in our lives. We must allow God to work through us, teach us, comfort us, and encourage us through the process of achieving financial freedom and establishing a legacy of living beyond ourselves.

> Honor the Lord with your wealth, with the first fruits of all your crops.
> (Proverbs 3:9, NIV)

What say you?

- In what area of your life are you investing your money?
- Do you pray and ask the Lord how you should spend your money?

EPISODE 47

Sacred Kiss *by Kristie K. McCrary and Melissa Young*

It was refreshing to hear this beautiful, educated, and even trendy, twenty-seven-year-old young lady share the story and testimony of how she made a commitment to God to wait until she was engaged before giving her next kiss. When she was only a month away from walking down the aisle, Melissa shared with me how and why she did it:

"A kiss is a commitment. Today, it's not used that way as much, but it should be. What do we do at the end of a wedding ceremony to seal our vows? We seal it with a kiss.

"When I realized this, I decided that I would wait until I was engaged to kiss again. I was tired of giving up part of myself without getting any results. Making out has become a trend, and once we kiss, often physicality goes downhill from there So many girls give away things that should be saved for the person that they will marry. If it takes compromise to get a guy, it will take compromise to keep him, because that's what the relationship is based on.

"Many guys get caught up in the moment and want to kiss and be affectionate, but they aren't ready to make the commitment that should come with that intimacy. It's a physical and emotional protection to wait for the right moment to kiss. It's like trying to drive a car but staying in first gear all of the time. It's just not natural or healthy. When you're dating, you constantly have to put on the breaks when God made us with the desires to keep going. That's why a kiss is so important.

"A kiss is intimate. It starts the fire. It starts everything. And one day it dawned on me how very special and intimate a kiss really was. It changed my life." Melissa told me.

I asked Melissa what advice she would give other young ladies on how to achieve this same goal.

She replied, "Make a commitment between you and God that it's going to be that way. Be accountable to someone for your actions and the commitment you've made, and don't ever place yourself in a compromising position that would encourage you to make a mistake. It's amazing to be able to look back without regret, with less emotional baggage, and with better communication with my finance—all because we waited until we had made that commitment to each other before we kissed. It's exciting to know that you've made it and you've done it right. It's like living out a testimony of God's faithfulness, because Doug and I are completely satisfied and in love, and we did it in a very unconventional way based on the standards of today."

I'm not saying that all single people should wait to kiss until they're engaged, because that's probably not for everyone. However, Melissa's thoughts make a tremendous amount of sense, and I can't help but respect her strength and commitment. It's vitally important to recognize the intimacy that a kiss brings so you will wait for the right moment and the right guy to share it with. It's too special to be given to just anyone.

For years, I have regularly said a prayer that I know has gotten me through some of the emotional times in my life, "Lord, line up my emotions according to your will. Nothing more and nothing less." Now, I can pray that every day, but unless I really mean it and yield my emotions and will to him, it will not be effective. On the other hand, if I completely submit to the Lord, I feel free and peaceful, knowing that he is my creator and he knows and wants the very best for me.

Today I am confident and assured that, because he is my father and creator, he will give me the best in his timing so I don't have to worry about it. All I have to do is be careful to guard my emotions and actions so that I'm able to wait for God to bring the best guy into my life in the healthiest way possible. I'm going to be patient and settle for the best.

> And now, my daughter, don't be afraid. I will do for you all you ask. All my fellow townsmen know that you are a woman of noble character.
> (Ruth 3:11, NIV)

What say you?

- Do you have someone in your life who keeps you accountable in your relationships and in your walk with Christ?

- Do you truly believe that you are special and that God has created you to experience an incredible and blessed romance with someone?

EPISODE 48
Is He the Only One? *by Judith Sallador*

In my first "real" Christian relationship, the guy I was dating was my everything. He seemed perfect in every way, and, because I loved Jesus and he loved Jesus, I thought we were meant to be. Our relationship deepened quickly, and within months, we were already talking about marriage.

My boyfriend, who was so serious about us and about God, decided to confess the skeletons he had been hiding in his closet. I had known him before he gave his heart to Christ, so I already knew about his sordid past and his previous relationships with other girls. Knowing all this and knowing that God had mercifully forgiven him, I wrote it off as his past and moved on.

Or at least I thought I did. Okay, at least I tried.

Days after his confession, I found myself sitting in class and thinking about our conversation. All I kept thinking to myself over and over again was, *I'm not the only one in his heart.*

The reality of this truth, whether past or present, made me sick to my stomach. *I'm not the only one in his heart.* Tears welled up in my eyes. *It was the past, God has forgiven him, and so have I, but … I'm not the only one in his heart.*

I know I'm not alone in feeling this way. In the book of Hosea, God asked his prophet to marry Gomer, an adulterous woman. In his sovereignty, God forewarned Hosea that Gomer would leave him several times for her other lovers, and yet God would have Hosea take her back time and time again. God used this as an example of his own love and faithfulness to the unfaithful nation of Israel. Regardless of Israel's sin and rebellion, God, with open arms has called out to Israel, trying to woo her back to her first love: him.

In the midst of my anger and confusion, God gently reminded me of his grace, saying, "I know and see your heart, and I know I'm not the only one. Despite all this, I still love you, and I want to be the only one." This made me stop and look at my life and at who or what I allowed to rule my heart. God wants me, all of me. Not that I deserve his love and grace by any means, but he sent his only son to die so I could be reunited in relationship with him once and for all.

The relationship I had with my boyfriend ended a few months later, but God had opened my eyes to a revelation. Every single day and every moment, God fights to win our hearts. Despite the circumstances we face—the busyness that crowds our life—he vies for our attention. Deuteronomy 4:24 states, "For the Lord your God is a consuming fire, a jealous God" (NIV). He desires intimacy with us. We claim we want him, but he's been yearning for us since the beginning of time.

Please understand this truth: the God who created the whole universe and the beauty of it all is madly in love with us. Will we let God be the only one in our hearts?

> But seek first the kingdom and his righteousness, and all these things will be given to you as well. (Matthew 6:33, NIV)

What say you?

- Is God the only one in your heart?
- How would you have personally handled the situation that Hosea found himself in?
- Are you willing to share your mate's heart with the Lord?

EPISODE 49
Heart Guard *by Sarah Billington*

The bible urges us to protect our heart, and then proceeds in explaining that it is the wellspring of life: "Above all else, guard your heart, for it is the wellspring of life" (Proverbs 4:23, NIV). Dictionary.com defines a wellspring as "a source or supply of anything, especially when considered inexhaustible." Then if our hearts are our wellsprings, then whatever we let into our hearts will show up in our lives.

God made women naturally emotional, compassionate, and more caring than men. Don't get me wrong; I'm not saying that men don't possess these important characteristics, but women tend to show them at a higher level, and that's what makes women such amazing creatures. In fact, most women show love to their friends, family, and coworkers on a daily basis, with no real effort on their part because it comes naturally.

So now that I have told you how amazing women are, let me break the bad news to you. Some of us tend to give our hearts away without thinking about the emotional consequence. What I mean by this is that some women get involved with men who are not exactly perfect—in short, we settle. Sometimes, we let men into our lives and hearts without really knowing who they are. Since women are emotional creatures, as we discussed earlier, any physical contact we have with a man is an emotional event. Whoever coined the phrase, "Don't let your guard down" must have read Proverbs 4:23.

You let your guard down when you trust people. Unfortunately, some men take this for granted and use women, which is why it is so important to guard your body as well as your heart. "Flee from sexual immorality. All other sins a man commits are outside his body, but he who sins sexually sins against his own body.

As I wrote once in a poem: "I need a love of my own, an adventure I can call home, not just something to condone." Do not settle. Guard your body. Most importantly, guard your heart. Most women want a prince charming, and that's understandable. If the shoe doesn't fit the prince, don't force it onto his foot, wait for the right one or the right foot!

> You are not your own; you were bought at a price. Therefore honor God with your body.
> (1 Corinthians 6:18–20, MSG)

What say you?

- Who have you given your heart to?
- Is it worth giving your heart to the wrong man rather than waiting patiently for God's best?
- Are you forcing your heart to love someone other than God?

EPISODE 50

Wait *by Heidi M. Pinon*

Wait.

No one likes to hear that dreadful word, but it seems to follow us. We do not like to hear it from anyone, because we know that we are not going to get what we want when we want it. Today, this message is almost unheard of. We live in a society in which we are used to getting things when we ask for them. Waiting longer than ten minutes for food—or anything else, for that matter—is a hardly tolerated inconvenience.

Fortunately for us, the world has adapted to our busy lives. We are spoiled with quick service, live television, fast-food drive-thru windows, microwaves, ice makers, instant coffee, breakfast bars, and countless other things that allow us to get things done quickly. God, however, has not adapted to our schedules. He works by his clock and his clock alone. He does not change, and he definitely does not give instant or microwavable answers to prayer.

It has always been extremely difficult for me to wait for what God has in store for me. One Christmas, for example, I convinced my mother to let me open some of my gifts a couple of days early. It was nice for the moment, but it was significantly disappointing when I only had one gift to open on Christmas morning.

Part of the growing process is the wait. Sometimes, waiting to get what we ask for is more beneficial than the prize itself. God faithfully blesses his children and provides for each of us. His priorities, however, are not always the same as ours. God sees the big picture. He wants us to develop our characters, learn patience, and be obedient to his word. Proverbs 3:5–6 says, "Trust in the Lord with all your heart and lean not on your own understanding; in all your ways acknowledge him, and he will make your paths straight" (NIV). The challenge is to put these words into practice.

Sometimes, the answers to our prayers are not for us to know. Part of waiting on God includes admitting that we cannot control some things and trusting in him to take care of those things. In most cases, we do not understand what God does, but once we trust in him, God faithfully gives us insurmountable peace.

A great biblical example of someone who trusted in and waited on the Lord is Joseph. The book of Genesis describes many trials that Joseph suffered, and through it all, he refused to stop trusting in the Lord. During his long wait, he became the leader God wanted him to be. God had given Joseph a dream, and he was willing to wait for God to make this dream come true.

God may not always do what we want him to do when we want him to do it, but he is always faithful. My father used to say, "When you are expecting God at twelve o'clock, he may not show up until eleven fifty-nine, but he will never be late." Jeremiah 29:11 tells us that God has a plan for each of our lives. His plans are better than anything we could ever imagine. Now the task that lies before us is to wait.

> "For I know the plans I have for you," declares the Lord, "plans to prosper you and not to harm you, plans to give you hope and a future."
> (Jeremiah 29:11, NIV)

What say you?

- Are you on your own agenda or are you on God's agenda?
- Do you wholeheartedly trust God during the waiting process?
- How long are you willing to wait for your miracle or blessing?

EPISODE 51

Settle for the Best *by Kristie K. McCrary*

The story of Isaac and Rebekah is one of the greatest romances in the Bible. Their story provides proof that God will never ask us to settle for anything less than the best.

Isaac was one of those responsible and submissive kids who most parents only dream about. He seemed almost flawless. To top it off, his father, Abraham, had become an incredibly wealthy man and would leave Isaac as the sole heir. Isaac was the very definition of "not a bad catch"—a kind, well-mannered, financially set, young gentleman who loves the Lord and has a great family. What more could a girl ask for in a mate?

Sixty-five years earlier, Abraham had left his homeland and settled in Canaan. Over time, Canaan had become an evil country, cursed by God. When Abraham called his senior servant to find a suitable mate for Isaac, he armed him with particular instructions: travel to their homeland and search for a bride with the same religious beliefs and background. This had to be the only plausible way to find the right girl.

During his journey, the servant stopped at a well just outside of the town of Nahor. He prayed to God to bring the right girl for Isaac to the well—he even asked that she would offer to water his camels. (See there, Christians have always asked for signs.) Before he concluded his prayer, Rebekah, a beautiful virgin, showed up, carrying a water jar (see Genesis 24:17–20).

Rebekah captured the heart of Abraham's servant with her outgoing personality, and he knelt and praised the Lord. Rebekah took the servant to meet her family, and they agreed that their meeting had occurred by the hand of God. It had to have been emotional to leave her family and homeland abruptly, to travel almost five hundred miles to marry a guy that she had never met. However, Rebekah recognized the hand of God and knew that he was giving her the best.

When the servant arrived back home with Rebekah, he went quickly to tell Isaac of the miraculous way in which the Lord had caused their paths to cross. Shortly thereafter, Isaac took Rebekah to be his wife, and he truly loved her.

This is as great of a love story as you will ever pay to see in the theater. God literally brought Isaac to Rebekah's doorstep through his servant. All that he required was for his servant to pray and wait for God's best.

If we could only comprehend how much God wants for us, we would never consider settling for anything less than the best. The importance of marrying a believer and allowing God to bring his choice for our mate into our lives is paramount. Outside of salvation, this is the most important decision we will ever make (see 1 Corinthians 7:39 and 2 Corinthians 6:14). For every authentic thing, there is a counterfeit. Be cautious; counterfeits often come along right before the real thing! Don't worry about encountering a fraud of what God intends for you. It will probably feel like everything is in place, but you will still have doubts. That is a warning from the Holy Spirit to wait and be patient. Good is the worst enemy of God's best.

Trust God to bring your Isaac or Rebekah into your life. Wait for his timing, and one day, you will wake up and discover that you have settled for the best.

> Trust God from the bottom of your heart; don't try to figure out everything on your own. Listen for God's voice in everything you do, everywhere you go; he's the one who will keep you on track.
> (Proverbs 3:5–6, MSG)

What say you?

- Could you be dating a counterfeit?
- Ask yourself this question, "Do I really want to spend the rest of my life with the person I am dating now? Do I truly believe we are compatible and will enjoy a successful and healthy marriage? Is God pleased with this relationship?"
- Do you pray before you enter into a dating relationship?
- Are you settling for the best?

EPISODE 52
Meet the Only Man Who Will Never Let You Down

by Kristie K. McCrary

You typically do the right thing and most people get along with you. You have a group of great friends, but despite the social get-togethers, the sound advice you provide, and the good deeds you do, you feel unsatisfied—like there is more out there. You have searched for that something in many places: relationships with others, parties, shopping, hanging out with a different crowd, maybe even drinking, drugs, or sex. So why do you still feel empty?

Have you ever left your house and felt like you forgot something? Well, that is the answer to feeling empty in life. You are without something, a relationship with Jesus Christ.

I talk to people—married and single—who struggle every day with disappointments and frustrations in their relationships. Whether the relationship relates to friendship, romance, work, or family, we're human and will eventually let someone down, even unintentionally. So it's important to reposition your thought process. Take the pressure off of human relationships and redirect that energy toward your relationship with the Lord. It will make all of the difference. Why? Because he's the only man who will never let you down.

Jesus the Christ became man—without ceasing to be God—in order to reveal the Father's nature and redeem man. He was conceived of the Holy Spirit and born of a virgin. Jesus is the substitution for our sins and he arose from the dead for our justification. Ascended into heaven, he is now exalted and seated at the right hand of God as our Mediator. He is fully God and fully man.

Jesus does love you, despite what you may have heard. He wants to have a relationship with you, but he will not invite himself in your life. You must let him in.

You have a life of important decisions to make: your major, your career, and your spouse. But no decision is more important than where you will spend eternity. Choose wisely and choose soon. Tomorrow is promised to no one, but God can make today the best day of your life.

If you are ready to accept the gift of eternal life through Jesus and you truly desire to invite him into your heart to be your personal Lord and Savior, then pray these words:

> Jesus, I know that I am a sinner and have been without you for too long. I am ready to make a change in my life and let you in as my personal Lord and Savior. I believe that you died for my sins and then rose from the grave so that I might have eternal life with you in heaven. I willingly repent of my sins and ask you to come into my heart and life. I trust you, God, to rule my mind, will, and emotions. Make me a better person and a child of God. Amen.

If you have just said this prayer and accepted Christ, we want to celebrate with you. If you have questions or concerns, please write to us. We want to encourage you in your walk with the Lord.

> I'll never let you down, never walk off and leave you. (Hebrews 13:5, MSG)

What say you?

- Do you believe in the reality of Heaven and Hell?
- If today was your last day on the earth, would you make it to Heaven or do you have doubts?
- What is possibly keeping you from surrendering your life to Jesus Christ?
- Even though God is perfect, do you ever struggle with the feeling that he might let you down? Why?
- Is the life that you are living worth missing Heaven for?

MOTION: High Velocity Devotions
is also available on compact disc.

For more information, e-mail or write to

Velo
PO Box 191949
Dallas, Texas 75219
www.velocyte.com
krismccrary@tx.rr.com

Velo is a 501c3 nonprofit organization recognized by the federal government and all financial gifts are tax deductible.

MEET THE CONTRIBUTORS

Kristie K. McCrary

Shari Askew . Sarah Billington . Amy Blevins . Courtney Bodine . Aunie Brooks . Melisa Conner. Julie M. Couch . Lesby Daniels . Angelica Garcia . Melissa Lagrone . Missy Lares . Keylee Lederer . Shelby Mace . Marla D. Monreal . Naomi Noy . Jennifer L. Oldham . Khia Page . Suzette Perlmutter . Heidi M. Pinon . Baileigh Robertson . Judith Sallador . Rachel L. Sarmiento . Lindsey Shipman . Priscilla Van Winkle . Cindy R. Wood . Kim Yarbrough . Melissa Young

Kristie K. McCrary

Founder and Executive Director

An English proverb espouses, "Never be afraid to try something new. Remember, amateurs built the ark; professionals built the Titanic."

Throughout her life, Kristie K. McCrary has found herself in those positions – places where most would feel alone and vulnerable, - but somehow she wasn't afraid to find new beginnings because of her faith and love for God.

Velo is a new beginning – not only for her, but also for young women across the country daring to try something new for God.

As founder and executive director of this progressive ministry, Kristie has been able to take the lessons from her life and mold them into practical, relevant tools for life. Her desire is to use those tools to help young women purposely and passionately gain momentum they need to reach their destiny.

Kristie has created momentum in the lives of today's women by teaching both truths from the Bible and intercessory prayer in small groups, speaking engagements such as Christ for the Nations Women's Conference, Mary Kay Events, and at churches across the country.

Additionally, she has featured her thoughts in national magazine publications including *Joyce Meyer Ministries Magazine Enjoying Everyday Life, Today's Pentecostal Evangel, CCSI Church CO-OP Magazine* and the *National Day of Prayer.*

Since Velo's inception in August 2004, Kristie has worked with other young women who have a sense of divine purpose and direction – they call themselves *Velocytes* – to co-author the ministry's first contemporary devotional in September 2006 entitled *Velo52 – High Velocity Devotions.* In July 2008, *Motion – High Velocity Devotions,* was published.

Kristie is a graduate of Oral Roberts University. Prior to founding Velo, Kristie owned and operated World Vision Travel, a full-service travel agency specializing in serving non-profit organizations and ministries around the globe.

Currently, she resides in Dallas, Texas looking for the next ship to set sail and hoping to bring many young women with her.

www.ingramcontent.com/pod-product-compliance
Lightning Source LLC
Chambersburg PA
CBHW020509100426
42813CB00030B/3171/J

* 9 7 8 0 5 9 5 4 8 9 6 1 9 *